The MAILBOX STORYTIME Arts & Crafts

Fun-to-make projects for 60 popular children's books!

- Builds enthusiasm for reading
- Makes use of everyday art supplies
- Includes step-by-step directions
- Invites student creativity

See page 95 for an index of titles and page 96 for an index of authors.

Managing Editor: Kimberly Ann Brugger

Editorial Team: Becky S. Andrews, Margaret Aumen, Diane Badden, Janet Boyce, Tricia Kylene Brown, Kimberley Bruck, Karen A. Brudnak, Elizabeth A. Cook, Pam Crane, Chris Curry, Roxanne LaBell Dearman, Beth Deki, David Drews, Brenda Fay, Ada Goren, Tazmen Fisher Hansen, Marsha Heim, Lori Z. Henry, Mark Rainey, Greg D. Rieves, Kelly Robertson, Hope Rodgers-Medina, Rebecca Saunders, Donna K. Teal, Sharon M. Tresino, Zane Williard

www.themailbox.com

©2013 The Mailbox® Books
All rights reserved.
ISBN 978-1-61276-367-5

Except as provided for herein, no part of this publication may be reproduced or transmitted in any form or by any means, electronic or mechanical, including photocopying, recording, or storing in any information storage and retrieval system or electronic online bulletin board, without prior written permission from The Education Center, LLC. Permission is given to the original purchaser to reproduce pages for individual classroom use only and not for resale or distribution. Reproduction for an entire school or school system is prohibited. Please direct written inquiries to The Education Center, LLC, PO Box 9753, Greensboro, NC 27429-0753. The Education Center®, The Mailbox®, the mailbox/post/grass logo, and The Mailbox Book Company® are registered trademarks of The Education Center, LLC. All other brand or product names are trademarks or registered trademarks of their respective companies.

Printed in the United States
10 9 8 7 6 5 4 3 2 1   HPS246117

Table of Contents

What's Inside 4

FALL

The Kissing Hand	5
Froggy Goes to School	6
The Apple Pie Tree	7
Ten Red Apples	8
Go Away, Big Green Monster!	9
Pumpkin Circle: The Story of a Garden	10
The Very Busy Spider	11
The Little Scarecrow Boy	12
Owl Babies	13
A Plump and Perky Turkey	14
Patterns and student activities	15

WINTER

The First Day of Winter	20
Gingerbread Friends	21
The Mitten	22
Owl Moon	23
Snow	24
Snowmen at Night	25
The Polar Express	26
Bear Snores On	27
The Emperor's Egg	28
Tacky the Penguin	29
Patterns and student activities	30

SPRING

Mouse's First Spring	35
The Carrot Seed	36
Planting a Rainbow	37
Miss Rumphius	38
Eggbert: The Slightly Cracked Egg	39
Make Way for Ducklings	40
Rain	41
The Runaway Bunny	42
The Very Hungry Caterpillar	43
Waiting for Wings	44
Patterns and student activities	45

SUMMER

In the Tall, Tall Grass	50
Jump, Frog, Jump!	51
Hello, Ocean	52
Down by the Bay	53
Fish Eyes: A Book You Can Count On	54
The Rainbow Fish	55
Blueberries for Sal	56
The Little Mouse, the Red Ripe Strawberry, and the Big Hungry Bear	57
Patterns and student activities	58

ANYTIME

Big Fat Hen	63
Big Red Barn	64
Brown Bear, Brown Bear, What Do You See?	65
Bunny Cakes	66
Chicka Chicka Boom Boom	67
Click, Clack, Moo: Cows That Type	68
Cookie's Week	69
Corduroy	70
Don't Let the Pigeon Drive the Bus!	71
The Foot Book	72
The Gruffalo	73
Harold and the Purple Crayon	74
Hattie and the Fox	75
If You Give a Mouse a Cookie	76
It Looked Like Spilt Milk	77
Little Blue and Little Yellow	78
Mouse Paint	79
My Friend Rabbit	80
Olivia	81
Russell the Sheep	82
Swimmy	83
Where the Wild Things Are	84
Patterns and student activities	85

Index 95

What's Inside

60 Literature-Related Art Experiences

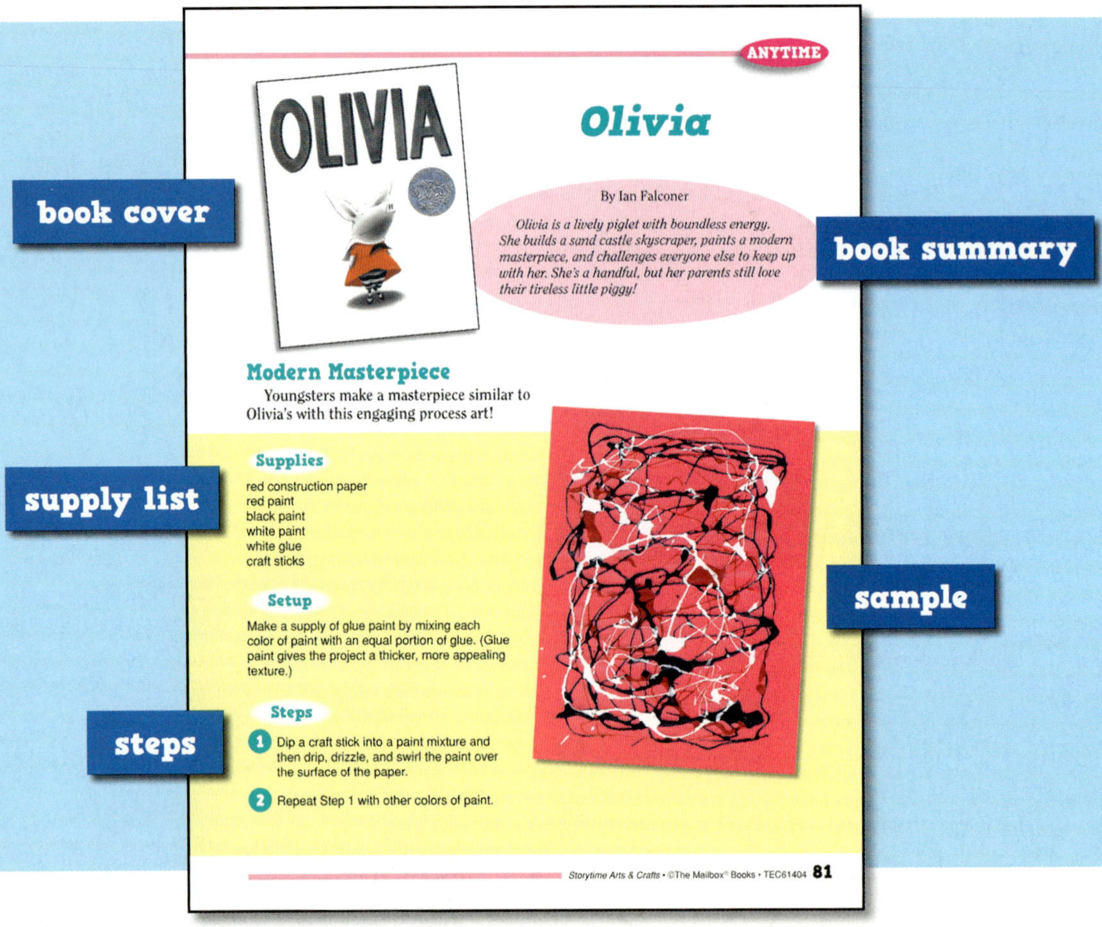

ANYTIME

Olivia

By Ian Falconer

Olivia is a lively piglet with boundless energy. She builds a sand castle skyscraper, paints a modern masterpiece, and challenges everyone else to keep up with her. She's a handful, but her parents still love their tireless little piggy!

Modern Masterpiece

Youngsters make a masterpiece similar to Olivia's with this engaging process art!

Supplies

red construction paper
red paint
black paint
white paint
white glue
craft sticks

Setup

Make a supply of glue paint by mixing each color of paint with an equal portion of glue. (Glue paint gives the project a thicker, more appealing texture.)

Steps

1. Dip a craft stick into a paint mixture and then drip, drizzle, and swirl the paint over the surface of the paper.
2. Repeat Step 1 with other colors of paint.

Storytime Arts & Crafts • ©The Mailbox® Books • TEC61404 81

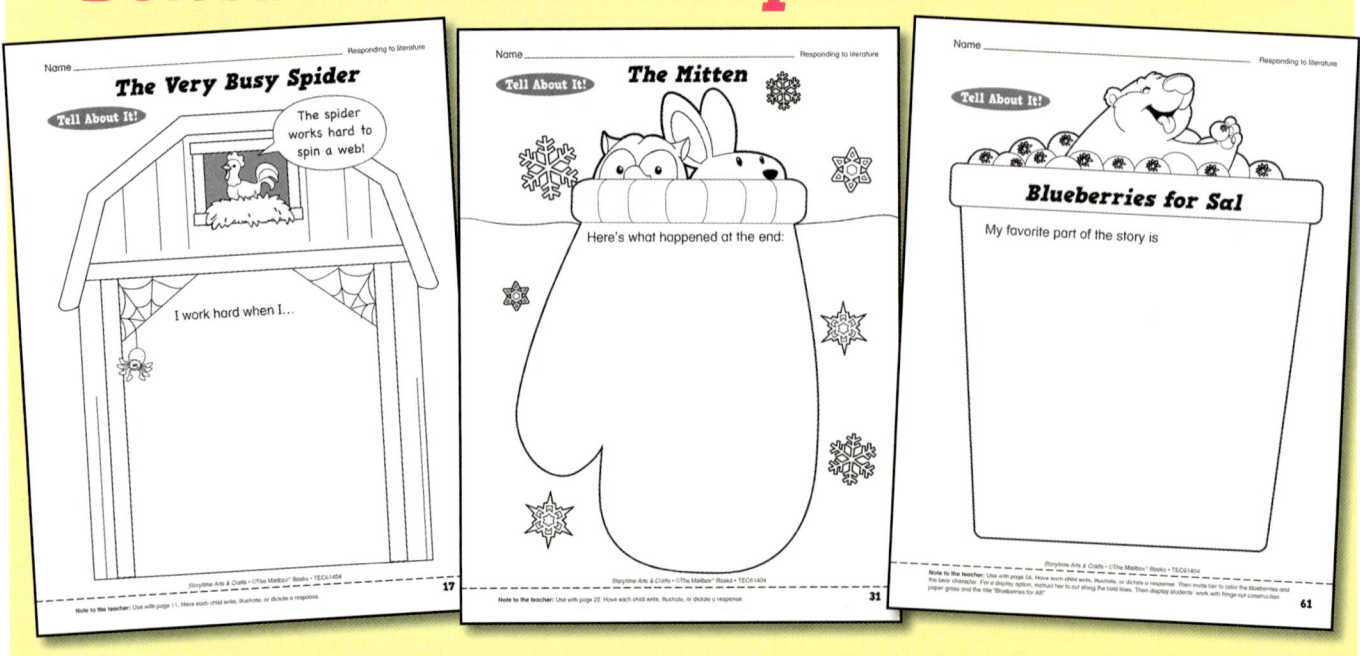

BONUS Literature Response Activities

FALL

The Kissing Hand

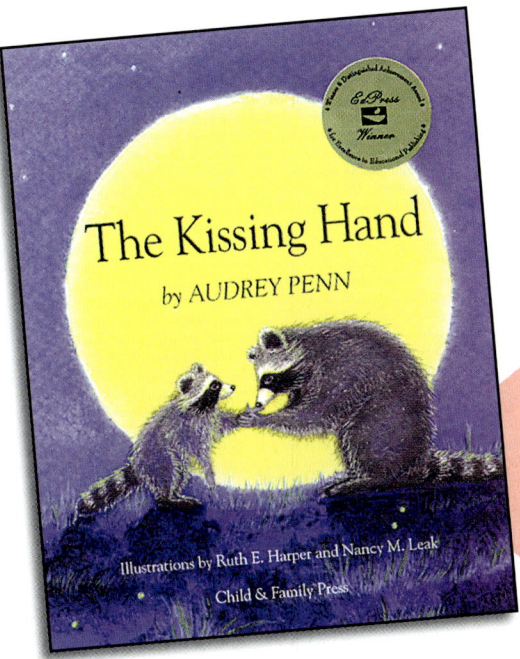

Written by Audrey Penn
Illustrated by Ruth E. Harper and Nancy M. Leak

Chester Raccoon doesn't want to leave his mother and go to school. So Chester's mother reassures Chester with a secret that helps him remember her love even when he is away from her.

A Little Love

Chester's mom kisses his hand and then has him press his hand to his cheek to feel her love. This Chester look-alike already has a bit of love on its cheek!

Supplies

paper plate
black construction paper ovals: one large (eye mask) and one small (nose)
2 gray construction paper circles (ears)
small red heart cutout
white and black construction paper scraps
gray paint   paintbrush
markers   scissors
glue

Steps

1. Paint the paper plate gray.
2. When the paint is dry, glue on the mask, ears, and nose.
3. Make two eyes from construction paper scraps and glue them in place.
4. Draw a mouth.
5. Glue the heart on the raccoon's cheek.

Tell About It! See page 15.

FALL

Froggy Goes to School

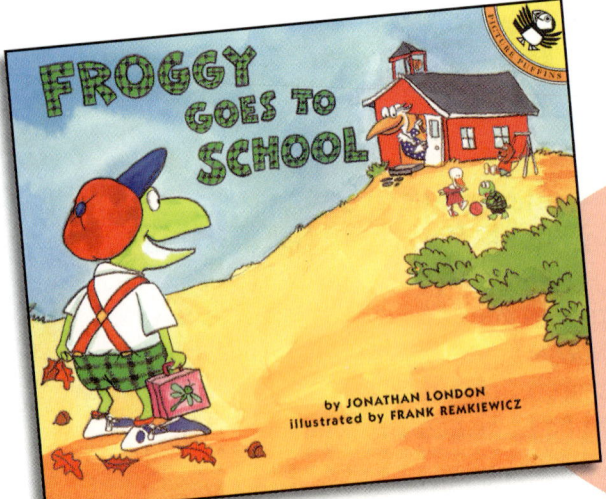

Written by Jonathan London
Illustrated by Frank Remkiewicz

Is Froggy nervous about his first day of school? Maybe a little, but with a "Zip! Zoop! Zup!" he's on his way. In the classroom, Froggy makes lots of mistakes and just can't sit still. So he uses his energy and his favorite song to teach everyone—including the principal—how to swim. What a great first day!

Flop, Flop, Flop!

Whenever Froggy and his family hop around, they make a fun sound—flop, flop, flop! Youngsters make the same sound when they make this fun process art!

Supplies

sheet of construction paper
shallow pan of green paint
black ink pad
black fine-tip marker

Steps

1. Dip your index finger and middle finger into the paint
2. "Hop" your fingers around the page while saying, "Flop, flop, flop!" so you sound just like Froggy!
3. Make black fingerprints on the paper.
4. Draw wings on the fingerprints so they resemble the flies that Froggy loves to eat.

FALL

The Apple Pie Tree

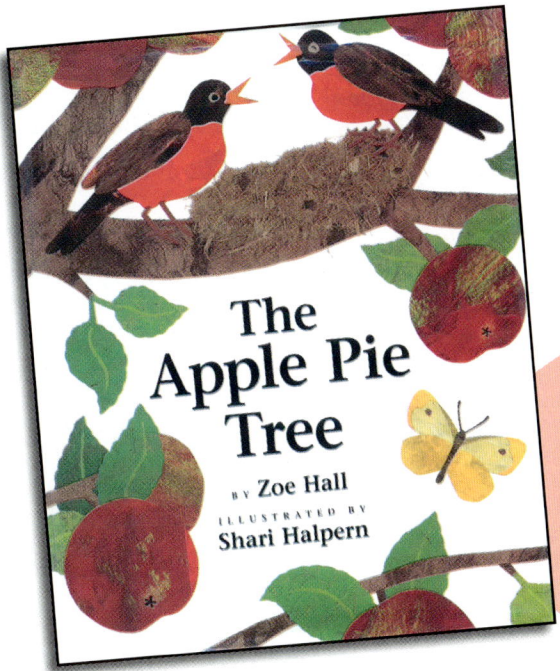

Written by Zoe Hall
Illustrated by Shari Halpern

Two young girls follow the changes to their own backyard apple tree through the seasons: from brown and bare to growing leaves to fragrant blossoms to tiny, green apples to big red fruit that's ready to be picked. It's time for apple pie! (And there's a recipe at the book's end!)

A Pleasing Pie

A secret ingredient makes this apple pie smell good enough to eat!

Supplies
apple, cut in half
cinnamon
paper plate
shallow container of red paint
brown crayon

Steps

1. Color the edge of the paper plate brown so that it looks like a crust.
2. Dip the flat side of an apple half in the paint.
3. Press the apple on the plate. Continue until a desired effect is achieved.
4. Sprinkle cinnamon on the wet paint, shaking off the excess.

FALL

Ten Red Apples

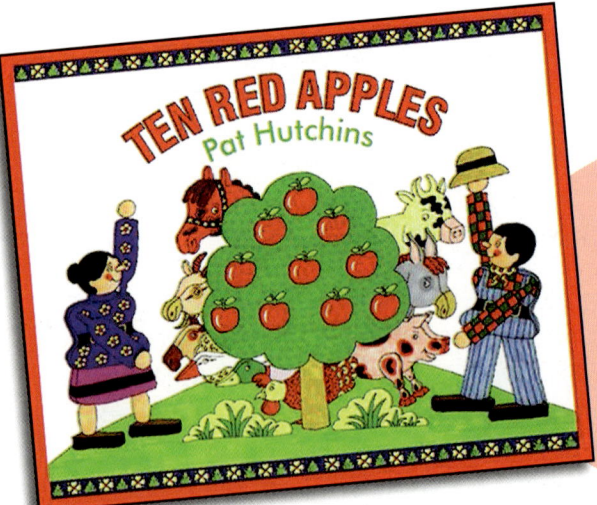

By Pat Hutchins

Fiddle-dee-fee, will there be any apples left in this tree? Rhyming, counting, repetition, and animal sounds lead readers through this book as the farm animals take the apples from the tree, one by one. With one apple left for the farmer but none for his wife, he spies another tree with ten apples, just in time to start again!

How Many Apples?

Youngsters put ten red apples on this self-standing apple tree. If desired, display the projects on a table to create a fabulous apple orchard!

Supplies
construction paper copy of page 16
large cardboard tube
10 red tissue paper squares
crayons
scissors
glue

Steps

1. Color the tree as desired.
2. Cut out the tree.
3. Crumple the tissue paper squares into small balls (apples).
4. Count the apples as you glue each one on the tree.
5. Glue the tube to the back of the tree.
6. When the glue is dry, stand the tree on a tabletop.

FALL

Go Away, Big Green Monster!

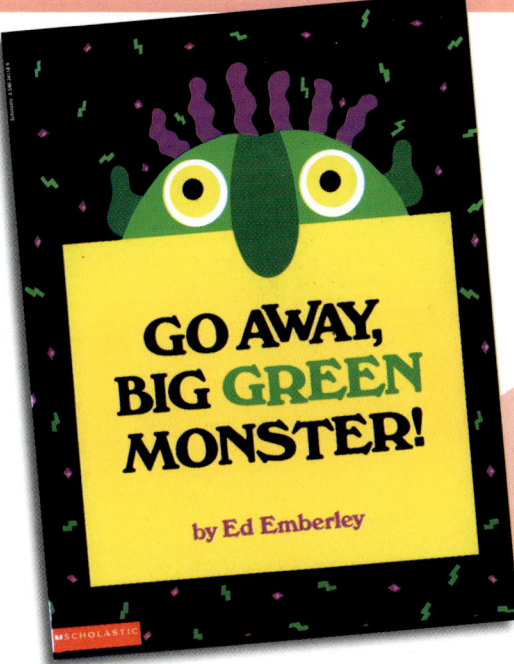

By Ed Emberley

Through descriptive text and bright colors, Big Green Monster grows with each turn of the page of this die-cut book. Then readers watch as he slowly disappears. "And don't come back! Until I say so."

A Disappearing Monster

Your students can make their own monsters go away whenever they want to!

Supplies

2 pieces of black construction paper
shape cutouts in a variety of colors
glue
tape
crayons

Steps

1. Use the shapes to make a monster on one piece of the black paper.
2. Add desired crayon details to complete the monster.
3. Place the other piece of black paper atop the piece with the monster.
4. Tape the top edges of the black papers together.
5. Flip up the top paper to make the monster appear. Flip it back down to make it disappear!

FALL

Pumpkin Circle: The Story of a Garden

Written by George Levenson
Photographs by Shmuel Thaler

"The pumpkin seed makes the pumpkin plant, and the pumpkin plant makes pumpkins." Full-color close-up views show the life cycle of a pumpkin—from seeds sprouting to full-grown pumpkins to the plant returning to the earth.

Round and Round

Review the life cycle of a pumpkin with youngsters as they make this three-dimensional craft.

Supplies

orange paper plate
green construction paper scraps
craft foam pumpkin seed
small piece of yellow tissue paper
small green pom-pom
large orange pom-pom
green and black permanent markers
scissors
glue

Steps

1. Cut a stem from the green paper scraps and glue it to the plate.
2. Glue the pumpkin seed below the stem.
3. Cut leaves from the green paper scraps and glue them to the plate.
4. Crumple the yellow tissue paper (flower) and glue it to the plate.
5. Glue the green pom-pom and the orange pom-pom to the plate.
   Teacher: Draw vines and arrows on the plate.

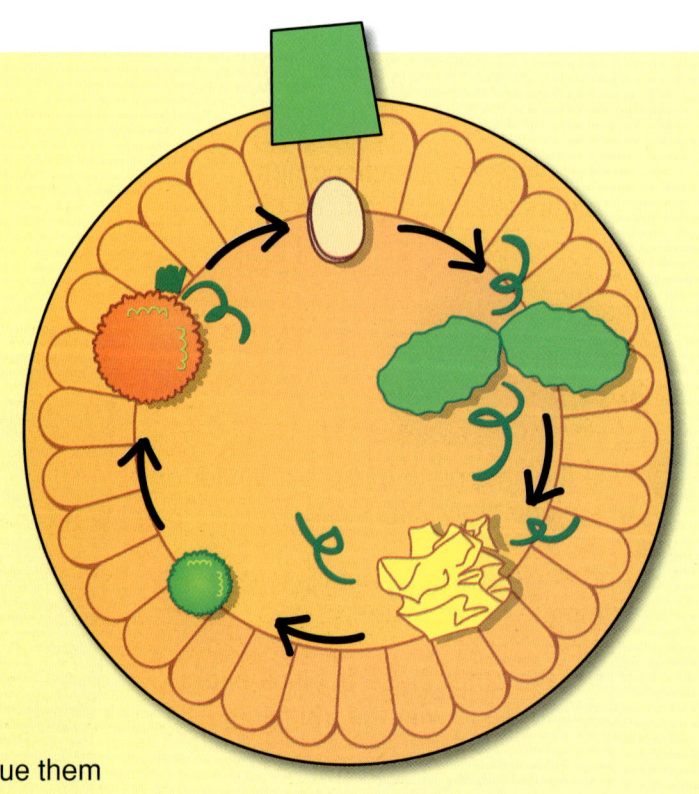

The Very Busy Spider

FALL

By Eric Carle

This industrious spider is busy spinning her web. Other farm animals ask her to play, but she knows if she doesn't finish the web, she'll have no dinner!

What a Web!

Youngsters create a tactile spider web similar to those in this book's illustrations.

Supplies

9" x 12" light blue construction paper
brown construction paper
white glue in a squeeze bottle
black pom-pom
black marker

Steps

1. Tear the brown paper into strips and glue them to the paper so they look like a split-rail fence.
2. Squeeze the glue to make a spider web within the fence posts.
3. When the glue is dry, glue the pom-pom to the web to make a spider body.
4. Draw eight legs by the spider body.

Tell About It!
See page 17.

FALL

The Little Scarecrow Boy

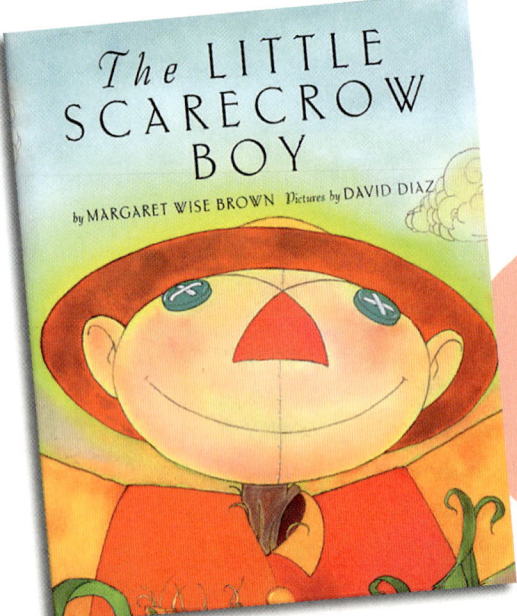

Written by Margaret Wise Brown
Illustrated by David Diaz

This little scarecrow boy is eager to learn the family business, but is he fierce enough to scare crows like old man scarecrow does? Little scarecrow boy decides to test his fierce faces against a crow. After several failed attempts, he frightens the crow and fills old man scarecrow with pride!

Make a Face!

Challenge youngsters to make their scariest scarecrow face to scare away a flock of crows!

Supplies

camera
circle punch
12" x 18" sheet of construction paper
black construction paper scraps
yellow triangles (beaks)
mini google eyes (or eye cutouts)
crayons
scissors
glue

Setup

Take a photo of each child making his scariest face and print out an enlarged copy. Cut out each child's head.

Steps

1. Glue the head to the sheet of paper. Draw a scarecrow body and hat as desired.
2. Draw cornstalks.
3. Punch black construction paper circles and glue them to the page.
4. Punch an identical set of circles and cut them in half. Glue the semicircles to the paper so they resemble wings.
5. Glue the beaks and eyes to the crows.

FALL

Owl Babies

Written by Martin Waddell
Illustrated by Patrick Benson

Three baby owlets awaken one night to discover their mother is gone. As they try to determine where she is, they become more and more worried about where she could be. Finally, the mother owl returns and assures her babies that she'll always come back.

Soft and Fluffy

Point out to students that while the mother owl in the story appears brown and feathery, the babies are white and fluffy. Then make this adorable craft.

Supplies

cotton batting
black construction paper
light brown construction paper strip (branch)
orange construction paper scraps
6 yellow circle cutouts (eyes)
orange and black markers
glue

Steps

1. Glue the branch to the paper.
2. Glue three balls of cotton batting above the branch.
3. Draw a pupil on each eye and then glue the eyes to the batting.
4. Cut three beaks from the orange paper and glue them to the batting.
5. Draw orange feet on the owls.

Tell About It! See page 18.

FALL

A Plump and Perky Turkey

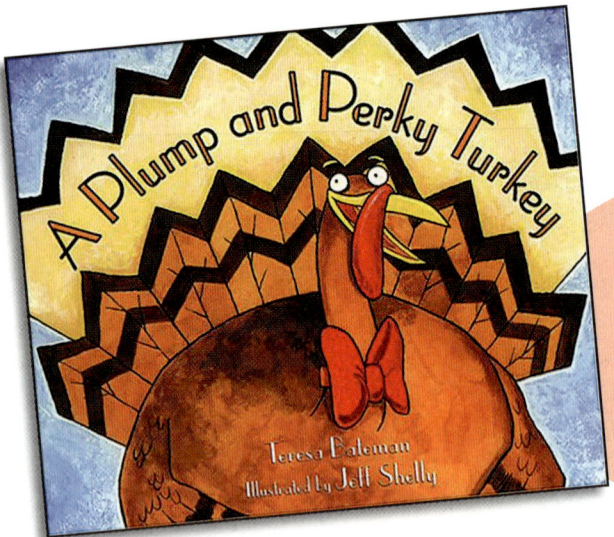

Written by Teresa Bateman
Illustrated by Jeff Shelly

The folks in Squawk Valley are missing a turkey for their Thanksgiving Day feast, so they attempt to lure one in by advertising for an artist's model for an arts-and-crafts fair. Pete the Turkey responds, poses, and then escapes with his "modeling fee" instead of becoming the main course!

Which Is the Real Pete?

Display these disguised turkeys below the title "Can You Find Pete?"

Supplies

copy of page 19
various craft supplies, such as feathers, pom-poms, and tissue paper scraps
glue
scissors
crayons

Steps

1. Use the craft supplies to disguise the turkey as desired.
2. Cut out the turkey.

Name _____ Responding to literature

The Kissing Hand

Tell About It!

At the beginning, Chester was…

At the end, Chester was…

Note to the teacher: Use with page 5. Have each child write, illustrate, or dictate a response.

Tree Pattern
Use with "How Many Apples?" on page 8.

Name _____ Responding to literature

Owl Babies

Tell About It!

This is where I think the owl mother went.

Note to the teacher: Use with page 13. Have each child write, illustrate, or dictate a response.

Turkey Pattern
Use with "Which Is the Real Pete?" on page 14.

WINTER

The First Day of Winter

By Denise Fleming

This snowman's best friend brings special gifts for each of the first ten days of winter. As each new item is introduced, the story counts back to the first gift, from ten salty peanuts for wintry toes back to a red cap with a gold snap. They're the trimmings for the most perfect snowman ever!

A Special Snowman

The boy in the story adds a detail to his snowman each day for ten days. Invite your little ones to do the same with these one-of-a-kind projects!

Supplies

9" x 12" white construction paper
variety of collage supplies, such as fabric scraps, ribbon, tissue paper scraps, and sequins
scissors
crayons
glue

Setup

Arrange the collage materials in an accessible location.

Steps

1. Draw a large snowman on the paper.

2. On the first day of winter, choose a collage material or gather crayons and add a desired detail to the snowman. Continue for each of the next nine days.

Gingerbread Friends

By Jan Brett

When Mattie is too busy for the Gingerbread Baby, the baby heads to the village to look for a friend. But the sweet treats at a bakery just stare at him and don't say a word. Discouraged, the Gingerbread Baby is chased home by some hungry creatures where he discovers that Mattie has cooked up a surprise: a cookie and candy village and lots of gingerbread friends!

A Tasty-Looking Trio

Making three gingerbread friends at once ensures that none of them will be lonely!

Supplies

tagboard gingerbread man tracer (pattern on page 30)
12" x 18" brown construction paper
assorted craft supplies, such as foam shapes, pom-poms, ribbon scraps, and fabric scraps
stapler
scissors
markers
glue

Setup

Accordion-fold the brown paper into three sections and staple it across the top and bottom.

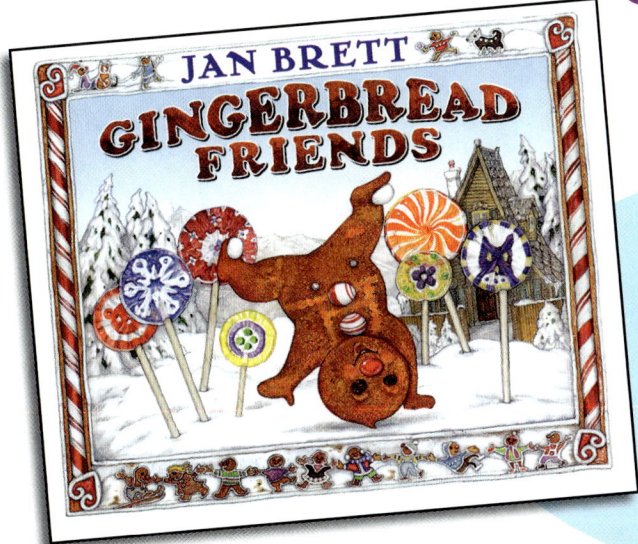

Steps

1. Trace the gingerbread man tracer on the folded brown paper.
2. Cut out the gingerbread man shape, making sure not to cut through the folds at the hands.
3. Unfold the paper and use the craft supplies to decorate the gingerbread friends as desired.

WINTER

The Mitten

By Jan Brett

Nicki has lost his white mitten in the snow. As he searches for it, a cast of animals, one by one, crawl into it to get warm, until a little mouse squeezes in next to a bear. With a tickle of the mouse's whiskers, the bear sneezes and sends the animals flying out of the mitten and the mitten into the air—right to Nicki!

In the Mitten

What is inside this mitten? Your youngsters will be eager to share!

Supplies

mitten
white construction paper
shallow pans of colored tempera paint
scissors
marker

Steps

1. Put the mitten on your hand. *(Hint: To keep hands clean, have the child wear a latex-free rubber glove under the mitten.)*

2. Gently press the mitten in the paint and then on the paper.

3. Repeat Step 2 with different colors of paint, overlapping prints as desired. Let the paint dry.

4. Cut a large mitten shape from the paper.

5. Think about what is inside your mitten. Dictate the words to be written on your project.

There is an elephant inside my mitten! It is really big.

Sara

Tell About It! See page 31.

Owl Moon

Written by Jane Yolen
Illustrated by John Schoenherr

Bravery, patience, and hope come into play as a little girl and her father tramp through the moonlit snow in search of a great horned owl. Responding to Pa's call, an owl lands on a nearby branch, its image caught in the light of Pa's flashlight, ending the nighttime adventure.

"Whoooo's" Hiding?

This owl's bright eyes will reveal its hiding spot in the frosty forest.

Supplies

9" x 12" black construction paper
green construction paper
white circle (moon)
2 yellow sticky dots (owl eyes)
glitter
scissors
container of glue
paintbrush
black marker

Setup

If youngsters need assistance making triangle cutouts, lightly draw lines on the green paper.

Steps

1. Cut triangles (trees) from the green paper.
2. Glue the trees to the black paper as desired.
3. Glue the moon in the sky.
4. Stick the two owl eyes in the trees.
5. Use the black marker to draw pupils on the eyes.
6. Use the paintbrush to dab glue on the page. Sprinkle glitter on the glue.

WINTER

Snow

By Uri Shulevitz

Will one or two snowflakes amount to anything? Nothing can dampen a young boy's growing anticipation of a snowstorm. And when the flakes gradually transform the gray buildings into a magical snow-covered cityscape, the boy and his dog know how to enjoy it with magical friends!

Snow-Covered City

Mixing shaving cream and glue gives this snow a realistic texture!

Supplies

12" x 18" blue construction paper
nonmentholated shaving cream
silver glitter
glue
gray crayon
large craft stick

Setup

To make snow, mix together equal parts of shaving cream and glue.

Steps

1. Use the crayon to draw a city like the one in the story.
2. Use the craft stick to cover the city with the snow mixture.
3. Add details to the city, such as doors and windows, with the craft stick.
4. Sprinkle glitter on the wet snow.

Snowmen at Night

Written by Caralyn Buehner
Illustrated by Mark Buehner

What do snowmen do at night that leaves them looking different from the day before? Snowman games, snowball fights, and snow angels are all part of the fun in this boy's imagination!

World's Best Snowball Fight

The snowmen in this story participate in some silly antics at night, including a snowball fight!

Supplies

black construction paper
brown construction paper strips
marshmallow
cotton swab
white paint
craft stick
crayons
glue

Setup

Insert the craft stick into one side of the marshmallow. Place the prepared marshmallow and the cotton swab with a shallow container of white paint.

Steps

1. Dip the marshmallow in the paint. Press it on the paper three times (one on top of the other) to make a snowman body.
2. Repeat Step 1 to make more snowmen. Let the paint dry.
3. Attach brown construction paper strips to make arms.
4. Dip the cotton swab in the paint. Dab it on the paper so it looks like snowballs being thrown by the snowmen.
5. Add desired details, such as facial features, hats, and scarves to the snowmen.

WINTER

The Polar Express

By Chris Van Allsburg

Transported by a magical train ride to the North Pole, a boy is chosen by Santa to receive the gift his heart desires. He chooses a silver bell from a reindeer's harness. Once home again, he learns that the ringing of the treasured bell can only be heard by those who truly believe.

A Special Gift

Students create the boy's gift from Santa with this unique craft.

Supplies

6" x 9" construction paper
large cork
cotton swab
gray and black paint
silver glitter
small piece of yarn
markers
glue

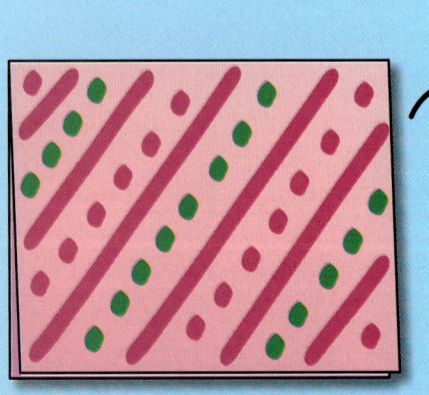

Steps

1. Fold the paper in half. Use markers to decorate the paper so that it looks like a wrapped gift.
2. Open the paper. Dip one end of the cork in gray paint.
3. Press the cork on the paper to make a print.
4. Dip the cotton swab in black paint and make a small *X* in the middle of the print. Sprinkle glitter on the wet paint.
5. Allow the paint to dry.
6. Glue the yarn to the top of the print so that the print looks like a jingle bell.

Tell About It! See page 32.

WINTER

Bear Snores On

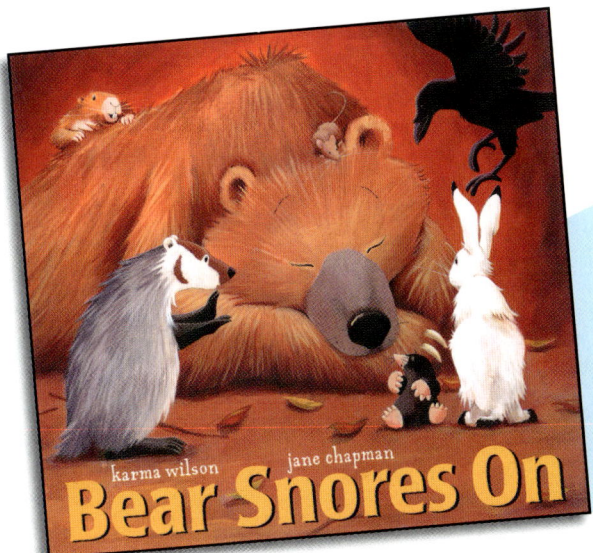

Written by Karma Wilson
Illustrated by Jane Chapman

On a cold winter night, a little mouse creeps into a big brown bear's cozy lair. Soon other animals join the mouse, and the party begins while Bear snores on. When Bear awakens, he's upset that he wasn't part of the festivities. But the other animals are quick to include Bear in the fun.

A Sleepy Bear

This textured bear's eyes open and close so it can appear to be asleep or awake, just like the bear in the story!

Supplies

two 2" brown construction paper circles (eyes)
two 3" brown construction paper circles (ears)
large paper plate
large black pom-pom (nose)
brown paint, thickened with flour
paintbrush
black marker

Steps

1. Fold the eyes in half. Open the eyes and draw pupils on the bottom half of each.
2. Paint the paper plate brown with the textured paint.
3. Glue the eyes, ears, and nose to the plate.
4. When the paint dries, flip open the eyes to show Bear awake and fold them to show him asleep.

WINTER

The Emperor's Egg

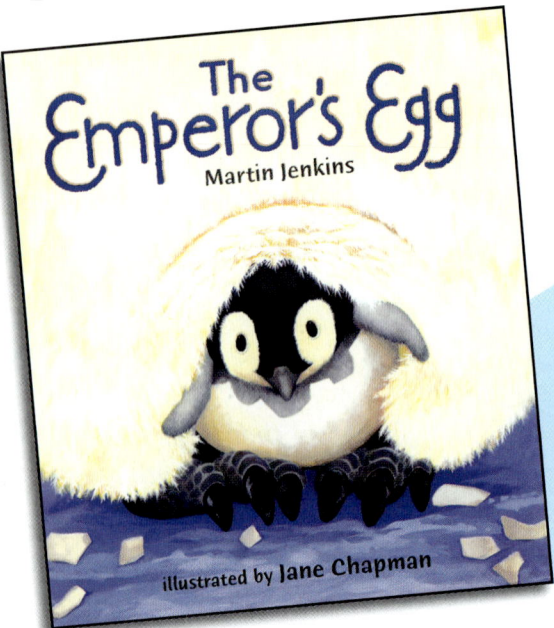

Written by Martin Jenkins
Illustrated by Jane Chapman

Meet some of the world's most devoted dads in this fact-based story about how male Emperor penguins care for their offspring. After the female lays the egg, the male keeps it warm in the freezing Antarctic cold by holding it on its feet for two months. Conversational text is sprinkled with penguin facts and engaging questions.

Time to Hatch

Paint this egg with corn syrup to give it a realistic look.

Supplies

white construction paper egg (pattern on page 33)
penguin chick cutout (patterns on page 33)
light corn syrup
brad fastener
crayons
paintbrush
scissors
glue

Steps

1. Color the chick.
2. Make a zigzag cut to separate the egg into two pieces.
3. Paint the egg halves with a thin layer of corn syrup to give them a shiny appearance. Let the corn syrup dry.
4. Glue the chick to the bottom piece and use the brad to secure the top piece as shown.

Tacky the Penguin

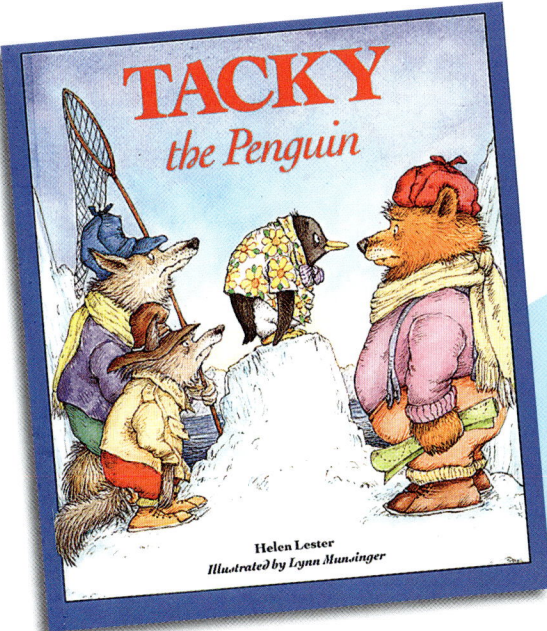

Written by Helen Lester
Illustrated by Lynn Munsinger

Tacky is a peculiar penguin—a bizarre bird. The other penguin's cringe over Tacky's differences—until the day the hunters come. Then his unpenguinlike antics convince the hunters that they are in the wrong place, and it becomes clear to the other penguins that an odd bird can be great to have around!

"Uniquely You" Shirts

One way Tacky expresses his personality is by wearing a unique shirt. Youngsters make their own wacky shirts with this project!

Supplies

12" x 18" construction paper
shirt pattern from page 34
various art supplies, such as fabric scraps,
   ribbon, glitter glue, and pom-poms
markers
scissors
glue

Steps

1. Use a variety of materials to decorate the shirt as desired.
2. Cut out the shirt.
3. Glue the shirt to the center of the construction paper.
4. Draw the rest of your body so that it looks like you are wearing the shirt.

Gingerbread Pattern
Use with "A Tasty-Looking Trio" on page 21.

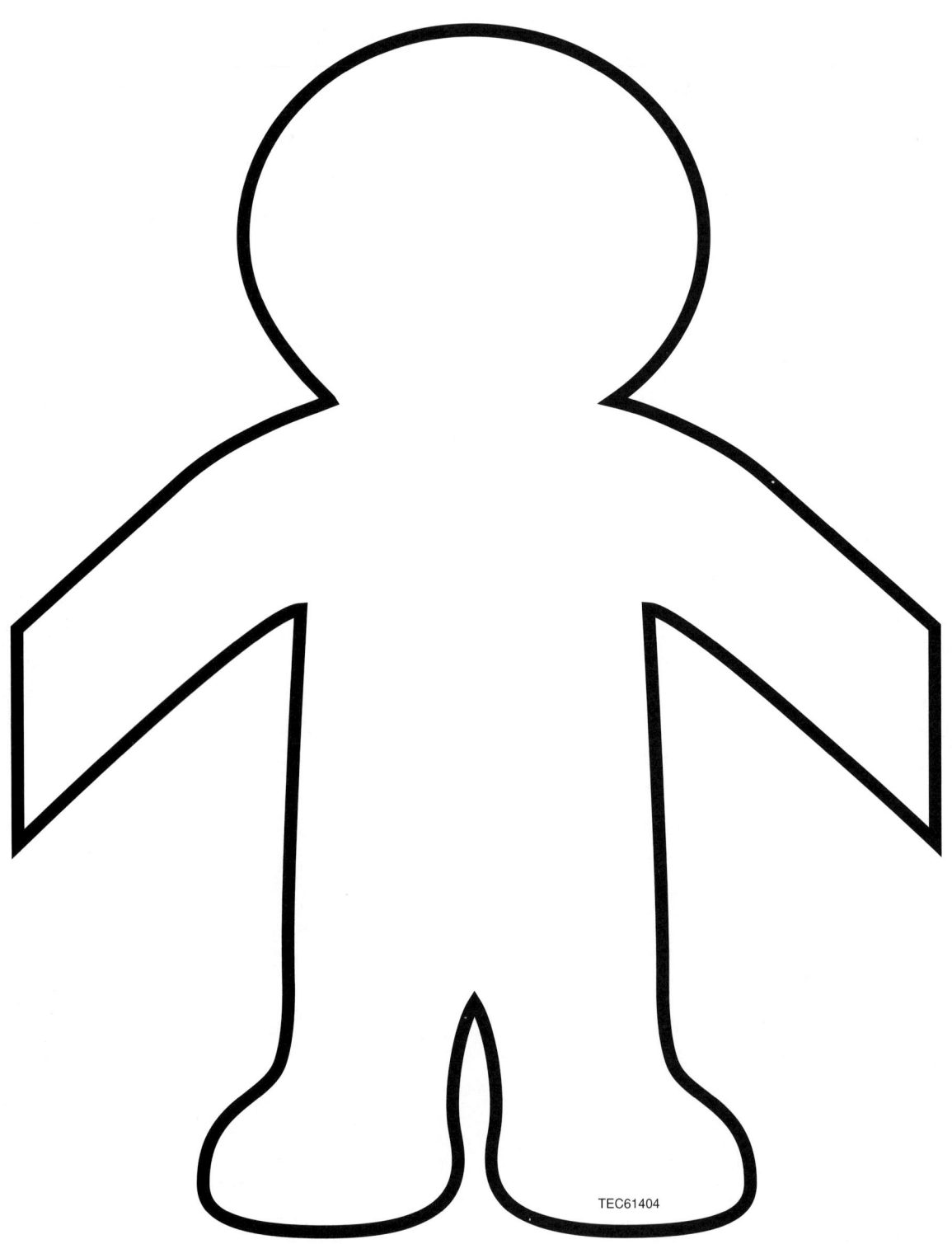

Name _____ Responding to literature

The Mitten

Tell About It!

Here's what happened at the end:

Note to the teacher: Use with page 22. Have each child write, illustrate, or dictate a response.

Name _____

Responding to literature

The Polar Express

Tell About It!

This is where the story takes place:

Note to the teacher: Use with page 26. Have each child write, illustrate, or dictate a response.

Storytime Arts & Crafts • ©The Mailbox® Books • TEC61404

Egg and Penguin Chick Patterns
Use with "Time to Hatch" on page 28.

Shirt Pattern
Use with "'Uniquely You' Shirts" on page 29.

Mouse's First Spring

Written by Lauren Thompson
Illustrated by Buket Erdogan

As Mouse and Momma venture out on a windy spring day, Mouse discovers a world full of new things! What could they be? Momma explains each one before the wind carries them away and then sweeps Mouse into Momma's loving arms.

SPRING

A Mouse in a Meadow

A plastic bottle is a perfect tool for making flower prints!

Supplies

gray construction paper copy of a mouse pattern from page 45
small plastic bottles
white construction paper
colorful medium-size pom-poms
tempera paint
green marker or crayon
scissors
glue

Steps

1. Cut out the mouse and glue it to the construction paper.

2. Press the bottom of a bottle in paint and then on the paper to make a flower. Repeat the process to make colorful flowers around the mouse.

3. Glue a pom-pom to the center of each flower.

4. When the paint is dry, use the marker to draw stems and leaves on the flowers.

SPRING

The Carrot Seed

Written by Ruth Krauss
Illustrated by Crockett Johnson

When a little boy plants a carrot seed, everyone tells him it won't grow. But he has faith in his plant, and he tends it carefully until it becomes a carrot worthy of a first prize at the state fair.

Pop-Up Carrot

This carrot craft makes a handy prop for retelling the story!

Supplies
- foam cup
- brown tissue paper squares
- construction paper carrot cutout
- green construction paper scraps
- jumbo craft stick
- paintbrush
- diluted glue
- glue

Setup
Cut a slit in the bottom of the cup wide enough for the craft stick to slide through.

Steps
1. Brush glue on part of the cup. Press the tissue paper squares on the glue. Repeat the process to cover the outside of the cup.
2. Tear small strips (leaves) from the paper scraps. Glue the leaves to the top of the carrot.
3. Glue the carrot to the craft stick.
4. Insert the craft stick through the slit. Push the stick up to make the carrot "grow."

Tell About It! See page 46.

Planting a Rainbow

By Lois Ehlert

This mother and child plant bulbs in the fall, order seeds in the winter, anticipate the sprouts in the spring, and choose seedlings in the summer to nurture a garden with a rainbow of colors.

Blooming Blossoms

With the squeeze of an eyedropper, colorful blossoms "bloom" right before your eyes!

Supplies

white paper towel
9" x 12" construction paper
3" x 12" brown construction paper strip
white or light brown yarn pieces
diluted tempera paint in several colors
eyedropper for each paint color
green marker
glue

Steps

1. Use the marker to draw flower stems with leaves on the paper towel.

2. Using the eyedroppers, squeeze paint on the paper towel above each stem.

3. Glue the paper towel to the construction paper.

4. Glue the paper strip below the flowers.

5. Glue yarn pieces below each stem so they resemble roots.

SPRING

Miss Rumphius

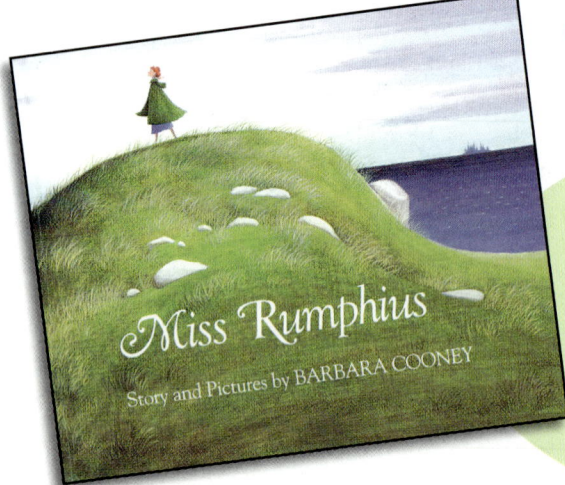

By Barbara Cooney

Alice dreams of going to faraway places and living by the sea, but her grandfather encourages her to also make the world a more beautiful place. How can she do that? The grown-up Alice—Miss Rumphius—fulfills her dreams and makes the world more beautiful by scattering seeds so that everyone can enjoy the beauty of colorful flowers.

Lovely Lupine

Inspire youngsters to make the world a more beautiful place with this artificial lupine!

Supplies

cardboard tube
light blue, pink, or purple tissue paper squares
green tempera paint
paintbrush
glue

Steps

1. Paint the tube (stem). Let the paint dry.

2. Crumple tissue paper squares and glue them to the stem, leaving a portion of the stem exposed at the bottom. *(If desired, display the resulting lupines with the title "Make the world a more beautiful place.")*

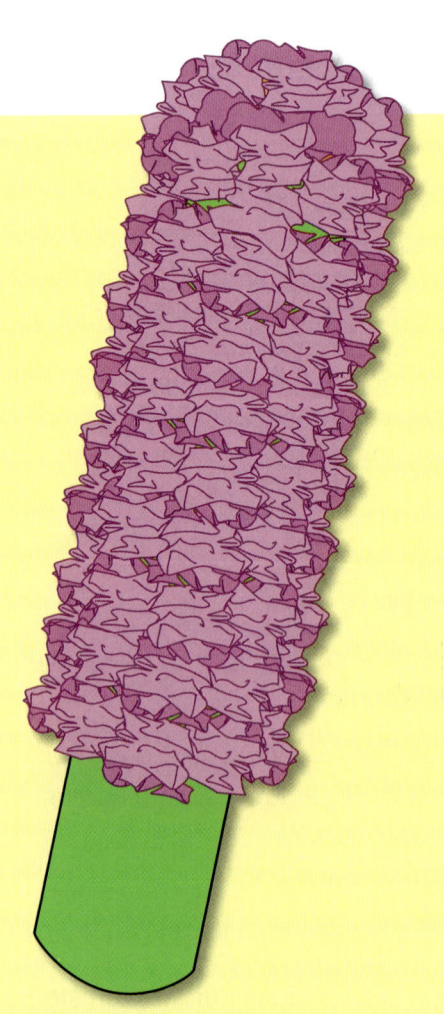

SPRING

Eggbert: The Slightly Cracked Egg

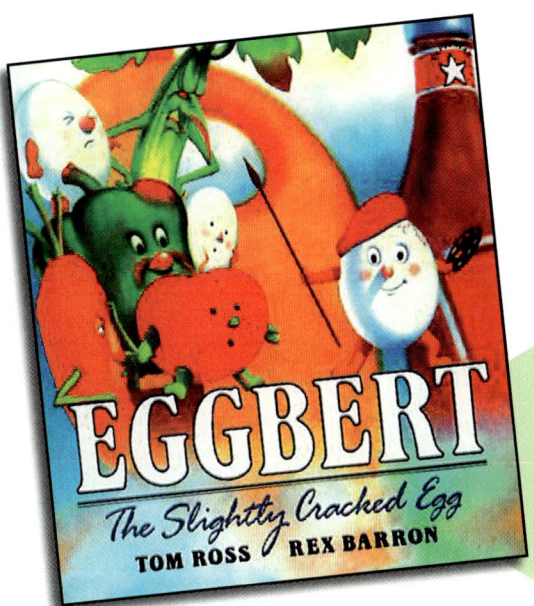

Written by Tom Ross
Illustrated by Rex Barron

Banished from the fridge because of a crack in his shell, Eggbert, an egg who's a talented painter, learns to accept his flaw and that it's okay to be different. Then he travels the world to see and paint famous sites with cracks.

Starlit Eggbert

Eggbert paints himself to blend in with his surroundings—like the night sky. This stellar craft resembles his masterpiece.

Supplies

copy of the patterns on page 47
unused toothbrush
white tagboard egg cutout
2 jumbo wiggle eyes
black and white
    tempera paint
sponge piece
glue

Steps

1. Sponge-paint the egg black.

2. Dip the toothbrush in white paint and then tap the brush against a finger to splatter the egg with paint.

3. Glue the wiggle eyes to the egg.

4. Color and cut out the patterns. Glue the pieces in place. *(If desired, attach a paper fence to a black background decorated with stars. Display the projects on the fence with the title "A perfect night covered with stars.")*

SPRING

Make Way for Ducklings

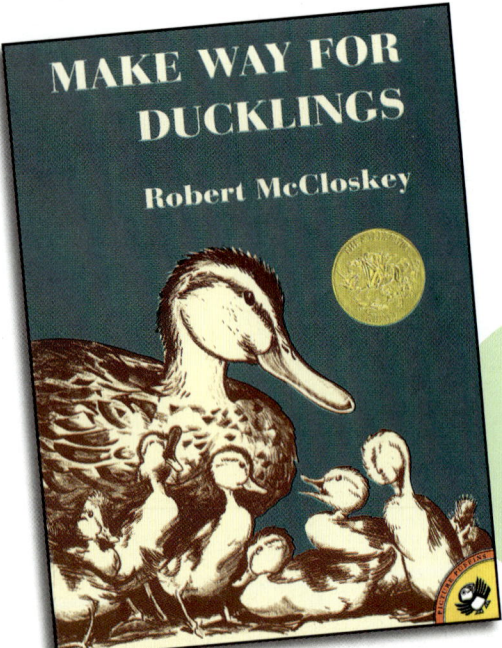

By Robert McCloskey

Mr. and Mrs. Mallard search on and on for a safe place to raise their family, finally landing in a river near Boston Public Garden. When the ducklings are big enough, it's time for the family to navigate the city streets to get to the pond in the Public Garden. With the help of a friendly policeman, their journey is a success!

Swimming With Mama Duck

Youngsters make ducklings swim with this pleasing process art!

Supplies

12" x 18" white construction paper
yellow pom-poms (ducklings)
foam paint roller
shallow container of blue paint mixed with white glue

Steps

1. Roll the paint roller in the paint mixture.

2. Apply the roller to the paper, making sure the paper is covered with paint so it resembles a pond.

3. Choose a duckling and pretend to make it swim in the pond. Then leave the duckling on the pond.

4. Repeat the process with several ducklings. Allow the mixture to dry, adhering the ducklings to the pond.

SPRING

Rain

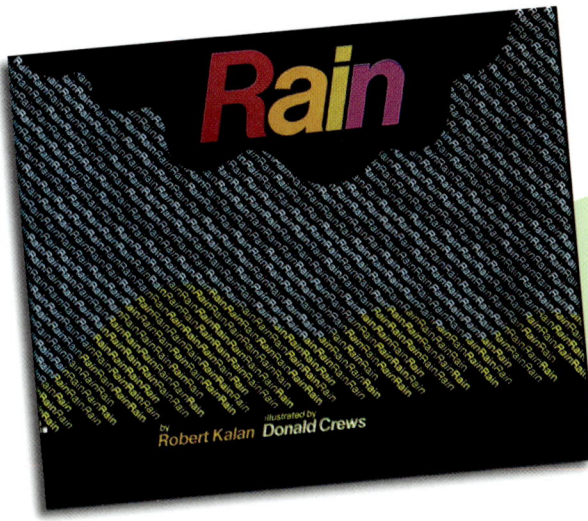

Written by Robert Kalan
Illustrated by David Crews

The blue skies and yellow sun transform to gray clouds and no sun and then—rain! Weather, colors, and a changing landscape are featured in this book.

Blue Skies to Rain

Watercolors and waxed paper transform a sunny scene into rainy weather, and vice versa!

Supplies
waxed paper
9" x 12" white construction paper
watercolors
squeeze bottle of gray tempera paint
small paintbrushes
tape

Setup
Tear off a ten-inch length of waxed paper. Fold the top inch of waxed paper under so it is only nine inches long.

Steps

1. Starting near the fold, squeeze gray paint along the top of the waxed paper. Use a paintbrush to swirl the paint so it resembles clouds.

2. Squeeze lines of gray paint below the clouds so they resemble rain. Let the paint dry.

3. Use the watercolors to paint a sunny outdoor scene on the construction paper.

4. Slide the scene upright into the fold of the waxed paper. Tape the fold to the back of the construction paper.

5. To change the weather scene, lift and lower the waxed paper.

SPRING

The Runaway Bunny

Written by Margaret Wise Brown
Illustrated by Clement Hurd

If this little bunny runs away, will his mother find him? You bet! What if he's a fish? She'll be a fisherman. What if he's a rock? She'll be a mountain climber. This adoring, protective mother promises she will always be there for him, because he is her little bunny.

Fishing for Bunny

Try fishing for this little bunny just like the mother bunny does in the story!

Supplies

white copy of the bunny pattern on page 48
12" x 18" light blue construction paper
orange carrot cutout
facial tissue
cotton ball (tail)
blue marker
scissors
yarn
glue
tape

Steps

1. Cut out the bunny pattern.

2. Glue torn facial tissue to the bunny so it resembles fur.

3. Use the marker to draw water lines on the paper.

4. Glue the bunny to the paper and the tail to the bunny.

5. Tape one end of a length of yarn to the carrot and the other end to the edge of the paper. Then "cast" the carrot into the water to try and catch the bunny!

SPRING

The Very Hungry Caterpillar

By Eric Carle

This tiny egg hatches into a caterpillar that goes on a weeklong eating spree! The caterpillar grows fatter and fatter with each passing day before cozying into a cocoon to undergo a brilliant change.

Colorful Creation

This idea results in a beautiful collage design that mimics the inside cover of the book!

Supplies

white construction paper
colorful tissue paper
white paint
wide foam brush
diluted glue
marker

Steps

1. Brush glue onto a portion of the paper.
2. Tear tissue paper and gently press it on the glue.
3. Repeat Step 2 until the paper is covered with colorful tissue paper.
4. Brush glue over the entire surface of the project. Let the glue dry.
5. Dip the bottom of the marker in the paint and randomly print dots on the project.

SPRING

Waiting for Wings

By Lois Ehlert

Follow the life cycle of four common butterflies—from tiny hidden eggs to hungry caterpillars that creep and then change into full-grown butterflies that spread their wings. Included are butterfly and flower facts and identification tips along with a guide to planting a butterfly garden!

Butterfly Finger Puppet

This wearable craft is sure to inspire plenty of butterfly play!

Supplies

white construction paper copy of
   the butterfly pattern on page 49
1" x 3" tagboard strip
shallow containers of tinted glue
pipe cleaner half
paintbrush
scissors
glitter
tape

Steps

1. Trim around the butterfly pattern.
2. Paint the butterfly with tinted glue.
3. Sprinkle glitter on the wet glue. Let the glue dry.
4. Shape the pipe cleaner so it resembles antennae. Tape the antennae to the butterfly.
5. Form a ring with the tagboard strip and secure it with tape. Tape the ring to the butterfly body. *To use the puppet, slide the ring onto your finger and manipulate the butterfly!*

Mouse Patterns
Use with "A Mouse in a Meadow" on page 35.

The Carrot Seed

Tell About It!

No one thought the carrot seed would grow, but…

Note to the teacher: Use with page 36. Have each child write, illustrate, or dictate a response. Encourage her to tear orange construction paper scraps into small pieces and glue them to the carrot. Then invite her to color the rest of the page.

Storytime Arts & Crafts • ©The Mailbox® Books • TEC61404

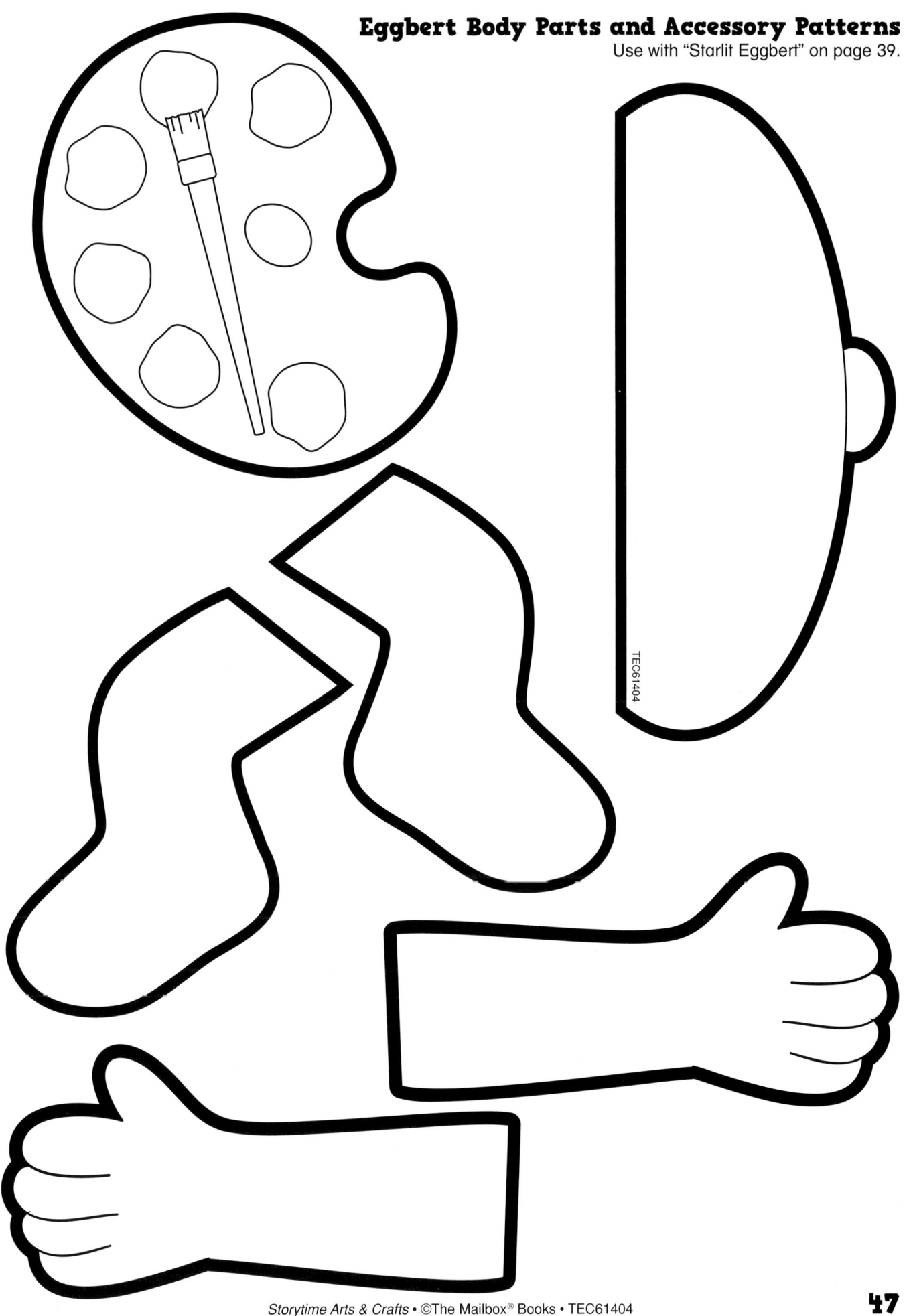

Eggbert Body Parts and Accessory Patterns
Use with "Starlit Eggbert" on page 39.

Bunny Pattern
Use with "Fishing for Bunny" on page 42.

Butterfly Pattern
Use with "Butterfly Finger Puppet" on page 44.

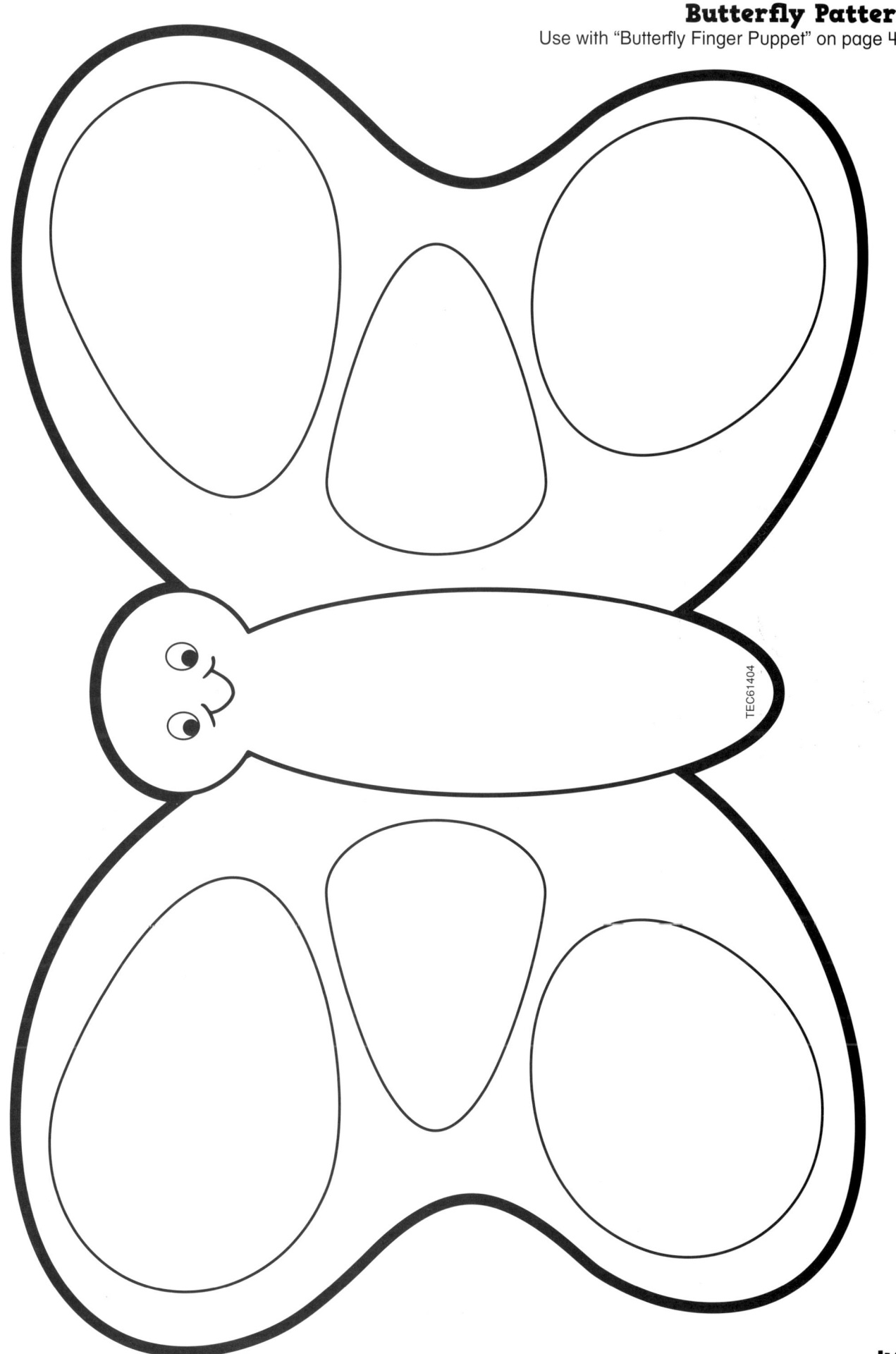

Summer

In the Tall, Tall Grass

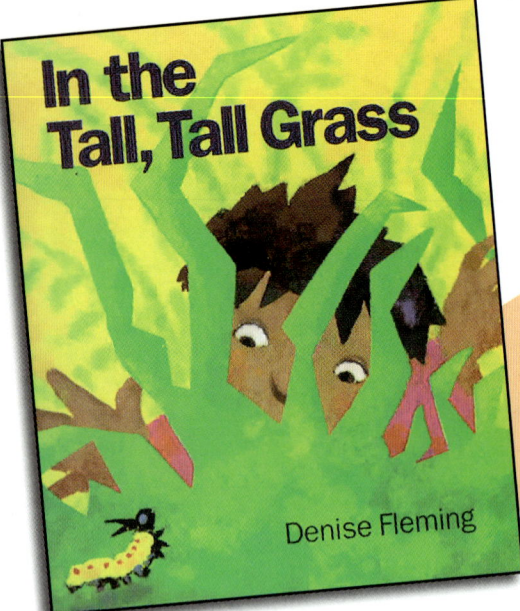

By Denise Fleming

A small boy discovers a caterpillar making its way through tall grass. If you were a fuzzy caterpillar, what would you see? This insect leads a backyard tour of animals—from ants to bees to bats and more—and their movements until the stars come out.

Snip and Seek

Discovering surprises in this grass is oodles of fun!

Supplies

9" x 12" white construction paper
9" x 12" green construction paper
tempera paint
ruler
markers
scissors
stapler
glue

Setup

Draw a horizontal line across each sheet of paper about three inches from the bottom.

Steps

1. Use the paint and your fingertip to make bug body prints and other small critters above the line on the white paper.
2. Use the scissors to cut long vertical slits in the green paper, stopping at the line.
3. Use the markers to draw details on the bug bodies and critters.
4. Form the project into a cylinder and staple it in place.
5. Glue the green paper to the cylinder as shown.

Jump, Frog, Jump!

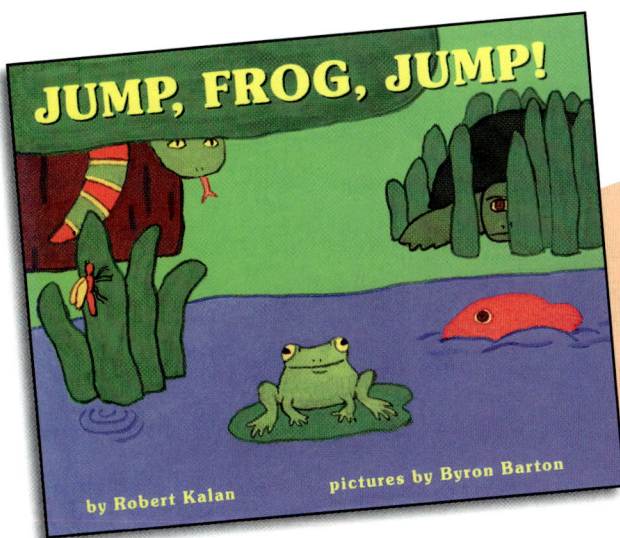

Written by Robert Kalan
Illustrated by Byron Barton

A frog, ready to gobble up a fly, finds itself jumping from other animals to avoid being on the other end of the food chain in this cumulative tale. It makes its final escape with the help of a boy. Jump, frog, jump!

Friendly Frog

Inspire lots of frog-hopping fun with this adorable puppet!

Supplies

2 paper plates
two 2" x 9" green paper strips trimmed as shown (legs)
two 1" x 4" green paper strips trimmed as shown (arms)
1½" x 6" tagboard strip
construction paper scraps
green tempera paint
paintbrush
stapler
glue

Steps

1. Paint the bottom of each plate.
2. Staple the edges of the plates together.
3. Fold the legs as shown. Glue the legs and arms in place.
4. Cut eye details, a mouth, and a tongue from the paper scraps and glue them in place.
5. Fold each end of the tagboard strip to make tabs. Glue the tabs to the back of the plate to form a handle that's roomy enough for fingers to slide through.
6. When the glue is dry, slide your hand into the handle and make your frog puppet hop about!

Summer

Hello, Ocean

Written by Pam Muñoz Ryan
Illustrated by Mark Astrella

A young girl sees, feels, hears, smells, and tastes her way through this ocean exploration. Poetic text mingled with scientific fact brings the ocean to life, with its "changing hue," "lion's roar," and "wet embrace" during the girl's visit to the beach.

Serene Seascape

A rolling pin, rubber bands, and paint help create this beautiful ocean scenery.

Supplies

white construction paper circle
light blue construction paper
white tempera paint
tray of blue tempera paint
crayons, including brown
cotton ball
rubber bands
glue
rolling pin

Setup

Wrap rubber bands around the rolling pin in a crisscross design.

Steps

1. Use the brown crayon to color the bottom edge of the blue paper.
2. Roll the rolling pin in blue paint and then across the paper. Repeat as desired.
3. Dip the cotton ball in the white paint and dab it on the paper to create the illusion of whitecaps and waves.
4. Use the crayons to color the circle so it resembles a beach ball.
5. Glue the beach ball to the paper.

Tell About It! See page 58.

Down by the Bay

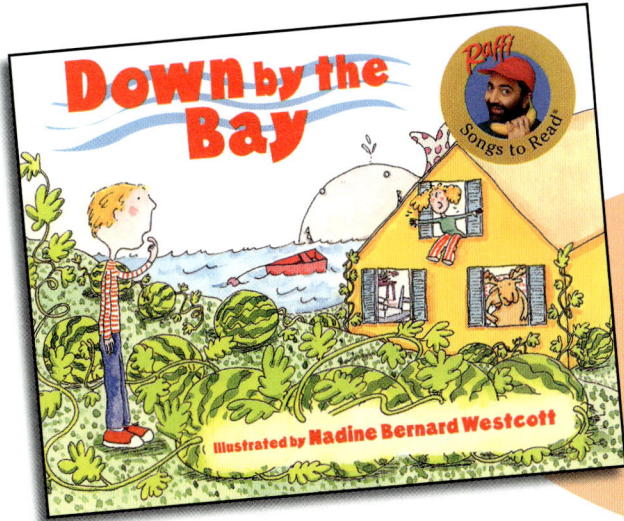

Written by Raffi
Illustrated by Nadine Bernard Westcott

Did you ever see a moose kissing a goose? How about a whale with a polka-dot tail? The lyrics from the song "Down by the Bay" are featured in this book along with all the characters—frantic mothers, busy children, unusual animals—and, of course, watermelons!

Watermelon Bay

Display one of these watermelon crafts as a visual incentive to create new verses!

Supplies

12" x 18" light blue construction paper
small oval-shaped potato halves
yellow construction paper semicircle
dark green and light green tempera paints
green yarn
small paintbrush
brown and yellow crayons
glue

Steps

1. Use the brown crayon to color the bottom half of the paper so it resembles soil.

2. Dip a potato half in dark green paint and then press it on the soil. Repeat the process to make several prints (watermelons).

3. Use the paintbrush to stroke light green stripes on the watermelons.

4. Glue a length of yarn (vine) to connect the watermelons.

5. Glue the semicircle (sun) to the top of the paper. Use the yellow crayon to draw sun rays.

Tell About It! See page 59.

Summer

Fish Eyes: A Book You Can Count On

By Lois Ehlert

Make a wish to be a fish—complete with fins, a tail, and scales—and count your way from one to ten with the vibrant colors and shapes on these fish. A small fish serves as a guide and introduces the concept of adding one.

Dot the Eyes

Hole-punch dots are the perfect source for making these fish eyes!

Supplies

sponge, trimmed into a fish shape
hole-punch dots and hole reinforcers
black construction paper
black tempera paint
crayons

Steps

1. Use the sponge and black paint to make fish prints on the paper. Let the paint dry.
2. Use a hole-punch dot and a hole reinforcer to make an eye on each fish.
3. Use the crayons to draw bubbles, waves, and other desired details.

The Rainbow Fish

Written by Marcus Pfister

The Rainbow Fish, with his sparkly scales, thought he was too beautiful to play with the other fish. But he was unhappy and didn't understand why the other sea creatures didn't like him. After seeking advice from the wise octopus, Rainbow Fish shares his shiny scales and discovers true happiness is on the inside.

Fancy Fish

This Rainbow Fish likeness is simple to make with shimmering results!

Supplies

white construction paper fish
ink pads in assorted colors
eye sticker (or cutout)
sequins
glue

Steps

1. Press your fingertip on an ink pad and then on the fish. Repeat the process until the fish is covered with colorful prints.

2. Stick the eye on and glue several sequins to the fish. *(For an eye-catching display option, mount blue cellophane [water], the fish crafts, and ocean-related details to a window.)*

Blueberries for Sal

By Robert McCloskey

Sal and her mother find lots of blueberries to eat and pick on Blueberry Hill. So do a bear cub and its mother. But as they're eating berries, Sal and the cub wind up trailing behind the wrong mothers! The mothers eventually discover the errors, back away, and search until they're reunited with the correct youngsters.

Bubbly Blueberries

Display these projects in a cluster to make a classroom blueberry patch!

Supplies

Bubble Wrap cushioning material with small bubbles
plastic bag crumpled into a ball
white construction paper bush shape
green and blue tempera paints
small paintbrush

Steps

1. Dip the bag in green paint and then press it on the bush. Repeat the process to cover the entire surface of the cutout.

2. Use the paintbrush to randomly dab blue paint on the Bubble Wrap cushioning material.

3. Place the bush atop the cushioning material painted-side down and gently rub your hand across the cutout.

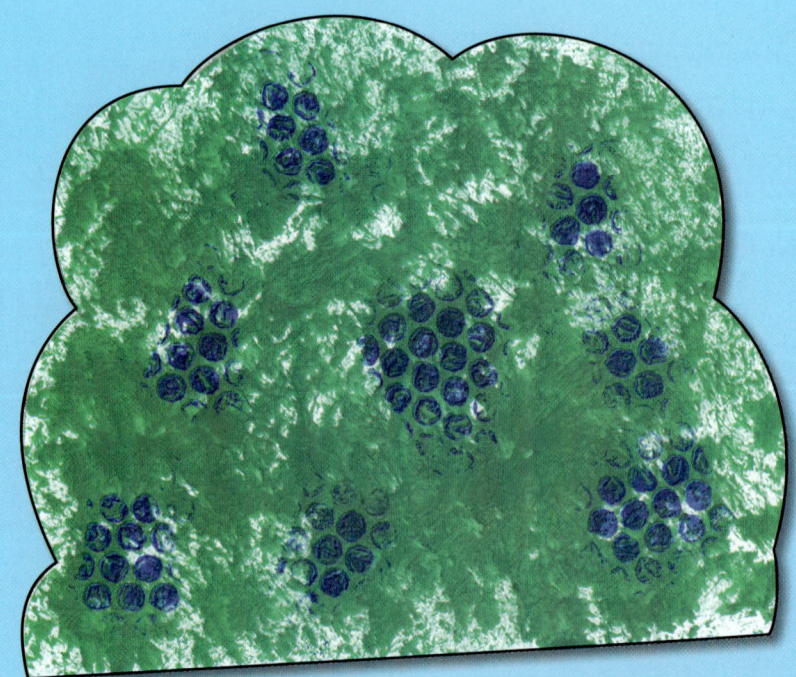

Tell About It! See page 61.

The Little Mouse, the Red Ripe Strawberry, and the Big Hungry Bear

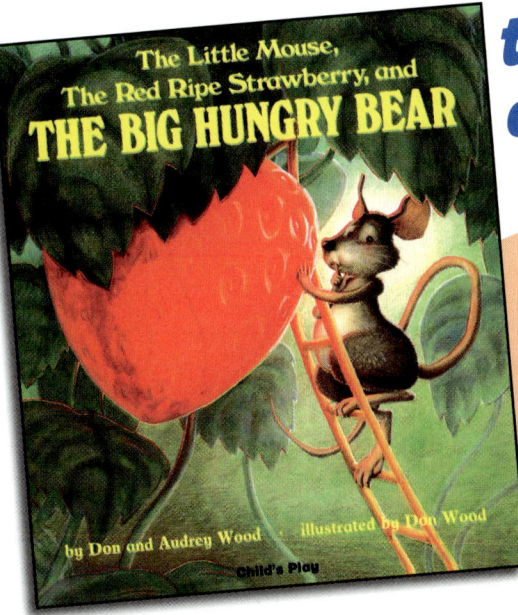

Written by Audrey Wood and Don Wood
Illustrated by Don Wood

How can this strawberry-loving mouse keep the big hungry bear from eating his giant strawberry? But is it the bear or the narrator who is really after the strawberry? The mouse attempts to protect his berry from the bear by disguising it and locking it up, and then he shares it with the narrator. That's one berry the bear will never get!

Strawberry in Disguise

This fruit may be incognito, but it sure smells like a strawberry!

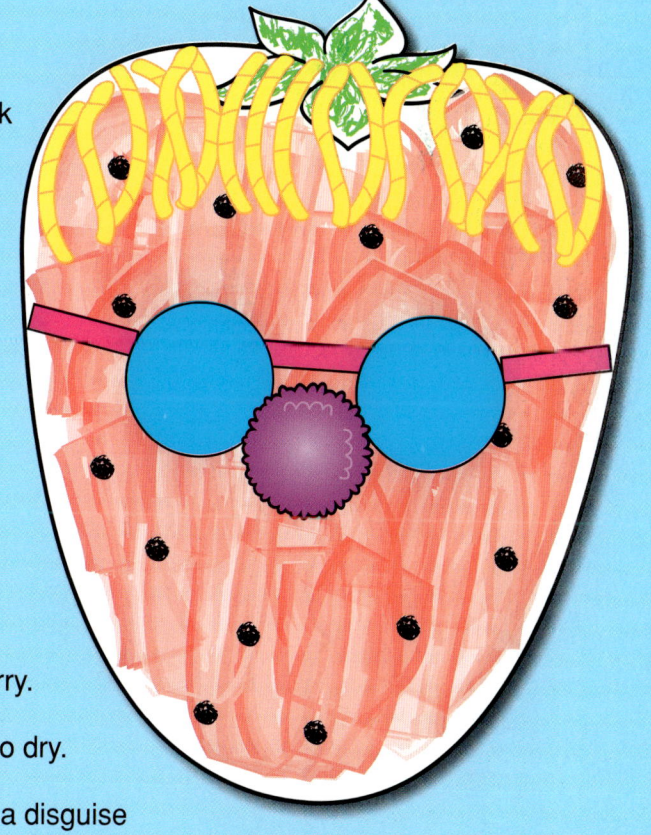

Supplies

white construction paper copy of the strawberry pattern on page 62
unsweetened strawberry-flavored drink mix
assorted craft materials
paintbrush
crayons, including black
scissors
glue

Setup

Mix the drink mix into a small cup of water.

Steps

1. Cut out the strawberry pattern.
2. Use the black crayon to draw seeds on the strawberry.
3. Paint the strawberry with the drink mixture. Allow it to dry.
4. Use the crayons, craft materials, and glue to create a disguise for the strawberry.

Storytime Arts & Crafts • ©The Mailbox® Books • TEC61404

Name _____

Responding to literature

Hello, Ocean

Tell About It!

The part that looks most fun is

Storytime Arts & Crafts • ©The Mailbox® Books • TEC61404

Note to the teacher: Use with page 52. Have each child write, illustrate, or dictate a response.

Name _____

Responding to literature

Down by the Bay

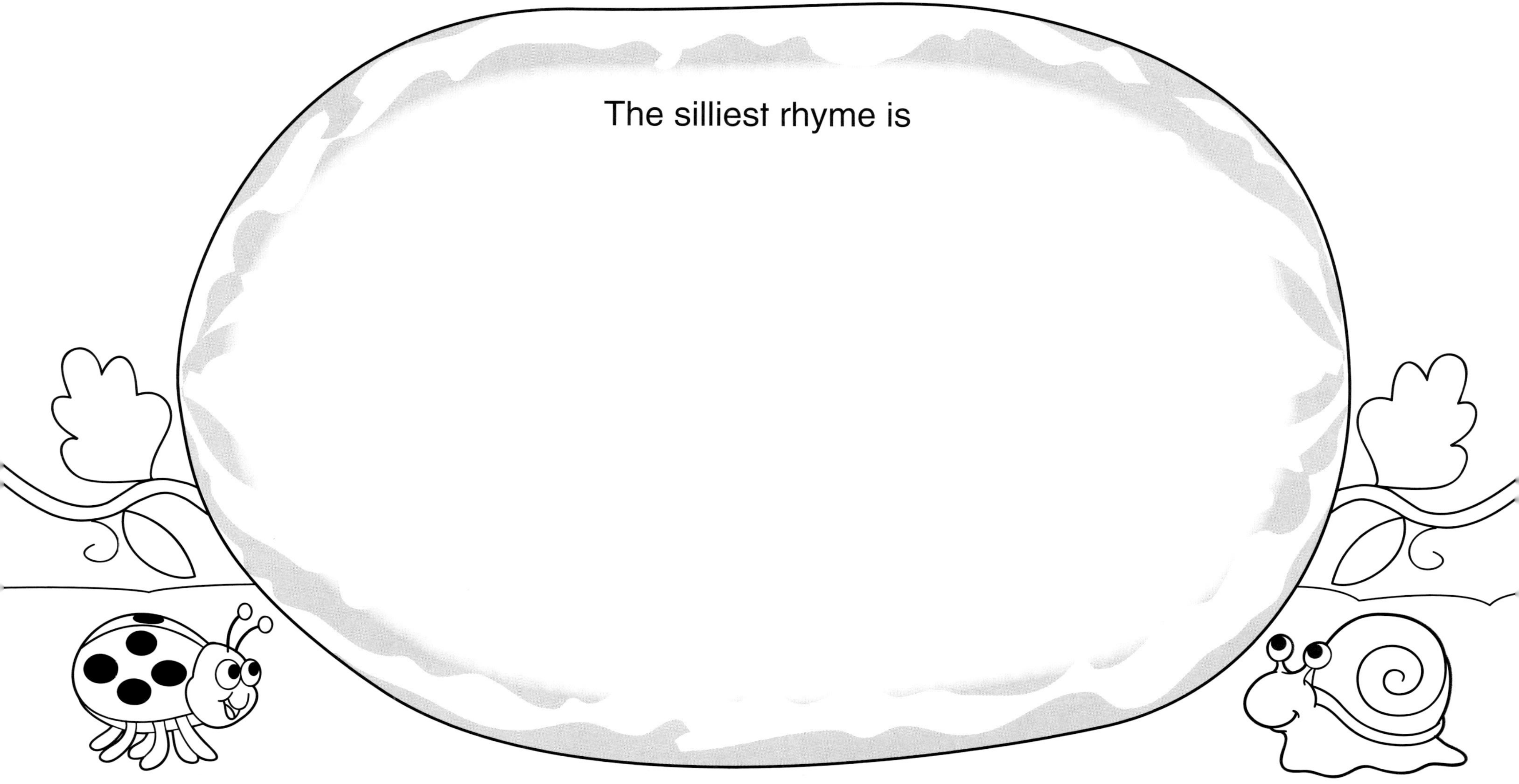

Tell About It!

The silliest rhyme is

Note to the teacher: Use with page 53. Have each child write, illustrate, or dictate a response.

Storytime Arts & Crafts • ©The Mailbox® Books • TEC61404

Name _____ Responding to literature

Rainbow Fish

Tell About It!

Here is what happened at the end:

Storytime Arts & Crafts • ©The Mailbox® Books • TEC61404

Note to the teacher: Use with page 55. Have each child write, illustrate, or dictate a response. Invite him to color the fish and the ocean scenery. Then have him glue one sequin to a fish.

Name _____   Responding to literature

Tell About It!

Blueberries for Sal

My favorite part of the story is

Storytime Arts & Crafts • ©The Mailbox® Books • TEC61404

Note to the teacher: Use with page 56. Have each child write, illustrate, or dictate a response. Then invite her to color the blueberries and the bear character. For a display option, instruct her to cut along the bold lines. Then display students' work with fringe-cut construction paper grass and the title "Blueberries for All!"

Strawberry Pattern
Use with "Strawberry in Disguise" on page 57.

Big Fat Hen

By Keith Baker

Newly hatched chicks, eggs, and bugs invite readers to count along from one to ten with the familiar counting rhyme. One, two, buckle my shoe… nine, ten, big fat hen!

From One to Ten

Youngsters practice this traditional rhyme and reinforce number identification skills with a simple project!

Supplies

number sponges from 1 to 10 (or stamps with ink pads)
orange and red craft feathers (hen's feathers)
sheet of brown construction paper
shallow pans of colorful tempera paint
glue

Steps

1. Find the number 1 sponge and press it in the paint. Then make a print on the paper.
2. Continue with numbers 2 through 10.
3. Glue the hen's feathers around the numbers.
4. When the paint is dry, touch each number while reciting the traditional rhyme.

ANYTIME

Big Red Barn

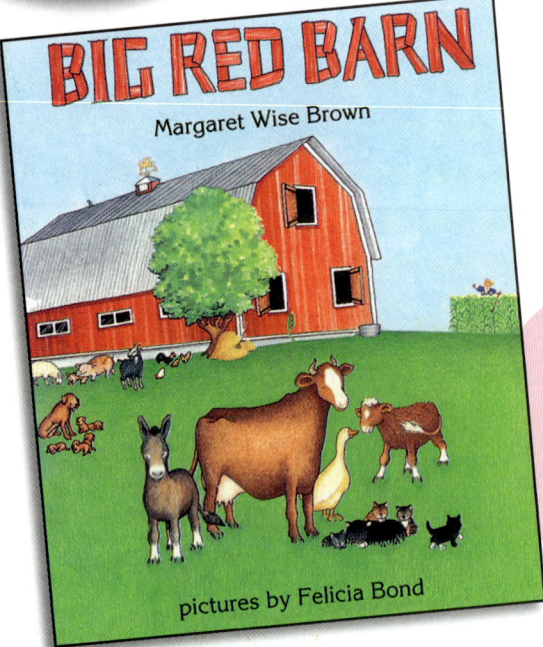

Written by Margaret Wise Brown
Illustrated by Felicia Bond

What will you find in the big red barn? Farm animals of all sorts—a pink pig, horses, cows, and more—coming out to enjoy the day. But when the sun sets, the animals return to the big red barn to sleep. That is, all the animals sleep except for the mice that play in the hay.

Who's in the Barn?

Youngsters will delight in revealing the hidden animals in this lift-the-flap craft!

Supplies

copy of the farm animal patterns on page 85
3" gray construction paper semicircle
six 3½" red construction paper squares
3" x 9" red construction paper rectangle
12" red construction paper square
scissors
crayons
glue

Steps

1. Trim the top of the construction paper square so it resembles a barn.

2. Glue the semicircle to one end of the rectangle. Glue the rectangle to one side of the barn so it resembles a silo.

3. Place glue on one edge of each square and then attach the squares to the barn to make flaps.

4. Use the crayons to draw desired details.

5. Color and cut out the animals. Glue each animal to the barn beneath a different flap.

Brown Bear, Brown Bear, What Do You See?

Written by Bill Martin Jr.
Illustrated by Eric Carle

What does Brown Bear see? Brown Bear answers, followed by Red Bird, Yellow Duck, Blue Horse, and other colorful animals in repetitive text until the end, where children take the final look!

"Bear-y" Colorful Reminder

Retelling the story is easy with this colorful memory jogger!

Supplies

two 3" brown construction paper semicircles (ears)
6" brown construction paper circle (head)
9" x 12" white construction paper
ruler
tempera paint (red, yellow, blue, green, purple, white, black, orange)
paintbrushes, one for each color
crayons, including an unwrapped brown crayon
glue

Setup

Draw eight one-inch rows on the construction paper.

Steps

1. Paint each row in the order shown to reflect the color order in the book. Let the paint dry.
2. Rub the side of the brown crayon on the head and ears.
3. Use the crayons to draw bearlike details on the head and ears.
4. Glue the ears to the head; then glue the head to the back of the paper as shown.
5. Draw a teacher and children at the bottom of the page.
6. Use the project to retell the story.

ANYTIME

Bunny Cakes

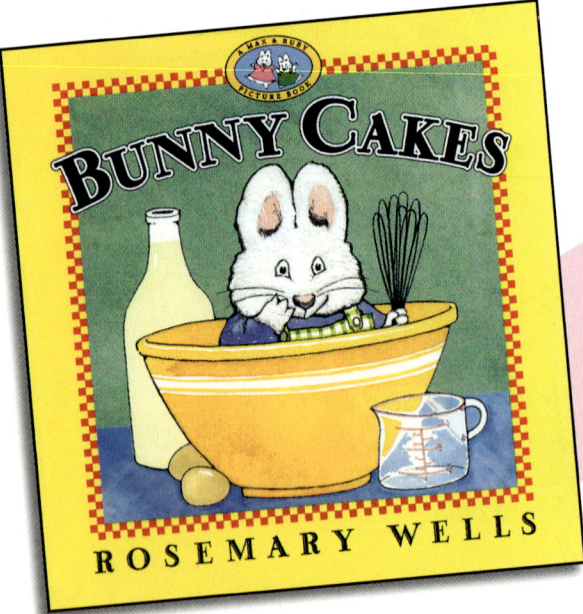

By Rosemary Wells

Max has the perfect ingredients for Grandma's birthday cake: earthworms topped with Red-Hot Marshmallow Squirters. But bossy older sister Ruby has her own ideas of what Grandma's cake and celebration should be like. Grandma finds both cakes and celebration ideas perfect for the occasion!

Earthworm Cake

The recipe for this homemade frosting consists of paint, soil, and glue!

Supplies

paper bowl
paper plate (optional)
brown tempera paint mixed with soil and glue
brown yarn pieces
small red pom-poms
paintbrush
glue

Steps

1. Turn the bowl upside down. Glue the bowl to the plate (optional).
2. Paint the bowl with a thick layer of the paint mixture.
3. Press yarn (earthworms) and pom-poms (Red-Hot Marshmallow Squirters) on the mixture.

Tell About It! See page 86.

Chicka Chicka Boom Boom

By Bill Martin Jr. and John Archambault
Illustrated by Lois Ehlert

"I'll meet you at the top of the coconut tree," one letter tells another, until all the letters of the alphabet weigh down the tree and end up in a big heap below it. After other letters race to their aid and the moon rises, with a "skit skat skoodle doot," A dares the letters to a race to the treetop again! Chicka Chicka BOOM BOOM!

Letter Characters

Have students take notice of the letter characters "Loose-Tooth *T*" and "Black-Eye *P*." Then encourage them to create their own unique letter characters!

Supplies

9" x 12" construction paper
craft materials, such as fabric, pom-poms, tissue paper, ribbon, and yarn
scissors
glue
crayons
black marker

Setup

Use the marker to write the first letter in the child's name on the construction paper.

Steps

1. Color the letter as desired.
2. Think of a way to give your letter a personality and accessories.
3. Cut and glue craft materials to dress up your letter.
4. Give your letter a name and write it on the paper. (Or dictate the name for an adult to write.)

Tell About It! See page 87.

ANYTIME

Click, Clack, Moo: Cows That Type

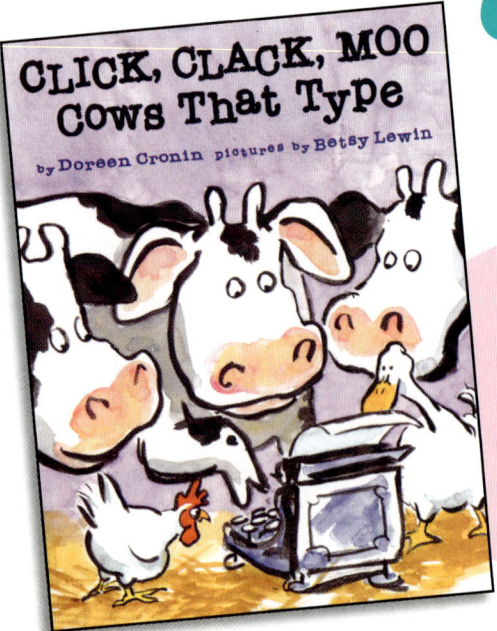

Written by Doreen Cronin
Illustrated by Betsy Lewin

The cows in Farmer Brown's barn are cold. When they discover an old typewriter, with a click, clack, moo, they type their demands. But Farmer Brown doesn't comply, so the cows go on strike, the hens join the strike, and a duck steps in as the mediator. A compromise is reached and all settles down on the farm—that is, until the ducks begin to type!

Duck at the Door

Who's at the door? Duck is delivering a message to Farmer Brown!

Supplies

newspaper
2" x 3" white paper rectangle
red construction paper folded in half lengthwise (door)
white construction paper
white feathers
orange and black markers
scissors
glue

Setup

Trace a child's shoe onto the white construction paper; then help her cut out the tracing (duck body).

Steps

1. Use a black marker to draw a doorknob on the folded paper. Unfold the paper.

2. Glue the body, wide-end down, to the right side of the paper.

3. Use the markers to add a beak, feet, and eyes; then glue a feather on the duck so it resembles tail feathers.

4. Snip individual letters (or a portion of text) from the newspaper to glue to the rectangle; then glue the resulting message below the duck's beak.

Tell About It!
See page 88.

Cookie's Week

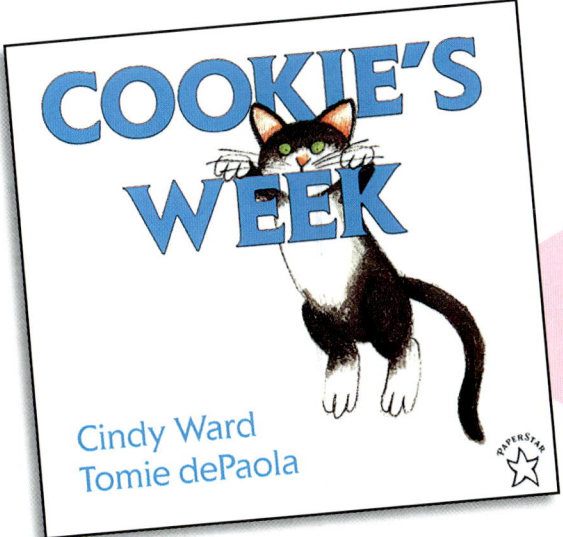

By Cindy Ward
Illustrated by Tomie de Paola

Cookie, a mischievous kitty, romps through each day of the week, leaving behind a trail of disasters!

Cookie's Closet

Fabric scraps come in handy for this cute craft!

Supplies

fabric scraps
sticky dot
black construction paper cat tail cutout
white construction paper cat paw cutout
brown construction paper folded in half and programmed as shown
scissors
squeeze bottle of glue

Steps

1. Attach the sticky dot to the folded paper so it resembles a doorknob.

2. Unfold the paper and squeeze glue onto the lower right half of the page.

3. Arrange fabric scraps atop the glue, trimming the scraps and adding glue as necessary.

4. Glue the tail and paw to the page so it looks like they're sticking out from under the fabric pile.

ANYTIME

Corduroy

By Don Freeman

Day after day, Corduroy waits with the other department store toys, eager for someone to take him home. When the overalls-clad teddy bear realizes that a missing button might jeopardize his chances of being purchased, he sets off in search of it. Happily, he discovers that a new friend likes him just the way he is—missing button and all!

Designer Overalls

Creative fashion is the highlight of these designer duds!

Supplies

white construction paper copy of the overalls pattern on page 89
tempera paint, in several colors
2 large craft foam circles
shape punches   construction paper scraps
paintbrushes   permanent marker
scissors   glue

Steps

1. Cut out the overalls pattern.

2. Paint the overalls as desired.

3. Use the permanent marker to draw an "X" on each craft foam circle so it resembles a button. Glue each button to the base of a strap.

4. Use the punches, paper scraps, and glue to embellish the overalls.

For a display option, mount several of the projects on a board or wall along with a teddy bear cutout wearing a pair of the overalls. Title the display "Corduroy Gets New Overalls!" Then periodically change the overalls until the bear has worn each pair.

ANYTIME

Don't Let the Pigeon Drive the Bus!

By Mo Willems

When the bus driver takes a break, the pigeon eagerly steps forward to take his place. But readers have been warned: don't let the pigeon drive the bus! The pigeon tries every trick in the book, being rejected each time until the bus driver returns. Maybe the pigeon can drive the tractor trailer instead!

Pigeon Portrait

Painting this character portrait leads to some creative thinking!

Supplies

round pool noodle
manila paper
white copy-paper speech bubble cutout
jumbo wiggle eye
light blue paint
yellow and black markers
glue

Setup

Slice off two circular pool noodle chunks. Slice one chunk in half. Write "If I can't drive the bus, maybe I can" on the speech bubble.

Steps

1. Dip the circular noodle chunk in the paint and press it on the paper to make the pigeon's head.

2. Turn the circular noodle chunk on its side and then dip the side in paint. Press it below the head to make the neck.

3. Dip the half noodle chunk in the paint and press it on the paper to make the body.

4. Glue the eye to the center of the head. Use the yellow marker to draw a beak and the black marker to draw legs. (Outline the beak in orange if desired.)

5. Write on the speech bubble to complete the sentence and glue the bubble above the pigeon.

ANYTIME

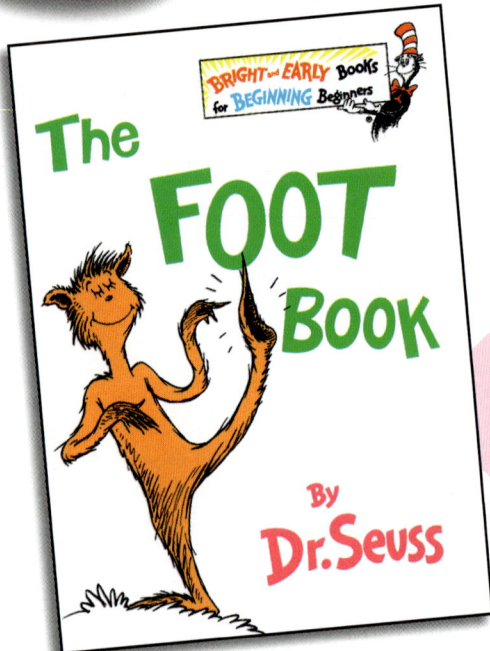

The Foot Book

By Dr. Seuss

Step in to opposites! Meet feet in all forms—left feet, right feet, wet feet, dry feet—and in different times and places—low and high, morning and night. It's a book of fancy footwork!

Left Foot, Right Foot

Colorful shoe tracings culminate in an abstract footwear design!

Supplies
pair of shoes
white construction paper
washable markers

Steps

1. Use a marker to trace one shoe onto the paper.
2. Move the shoe to a different position and trace it with a different marker.
3. Repeat Step 2 several times.
4. Repeat Steps 1 through 3 using the other shoe.

The Gruffalo

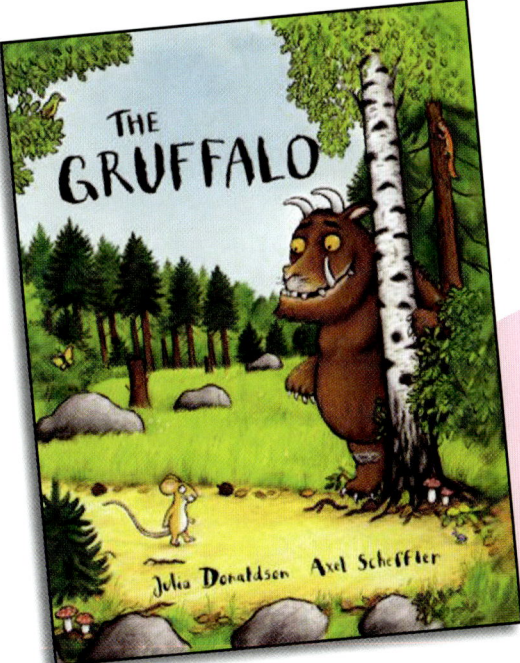

Written by Julia Donaldson
Illustrated by Axel Scheffler

The little mouse knows he'd be a tasty treat for animals in the deep dark wood, so he makes up a fearsome gruffalo to scare away a fox, an owl, and a snake. But when he's confronted with the terrible creature of his imagination, he tricks it as well, allowing him to enjoy his nut lunch in peace.

My Very Own Gruffalo

This fun craft results in a gruffalo with a personal touch!

Supplies

tagboard head cutout
4 tagboard strips (arms and legs)
large paper plate (body)
craft materials, such as white craft foam scraps, construction paper scraps, yarn, pom-poms
tempera paint   paintbrush
markers   stapler
scissors   glue

Steps

1. Paint the body.
2. Use the markers, craft materials, and glue to decorate the head as desired.
3. Staple the head, arms, and legs to the body.
4. Glue pieces of yarn to the body, arms, and legs. Glue on a yarn tail.
5. Use the scissors to snip small craft foam claws. Glue the claws to the hands and feet.

Tell About It! See page 90.

ANYTIME

Harold and the Purple Crayon

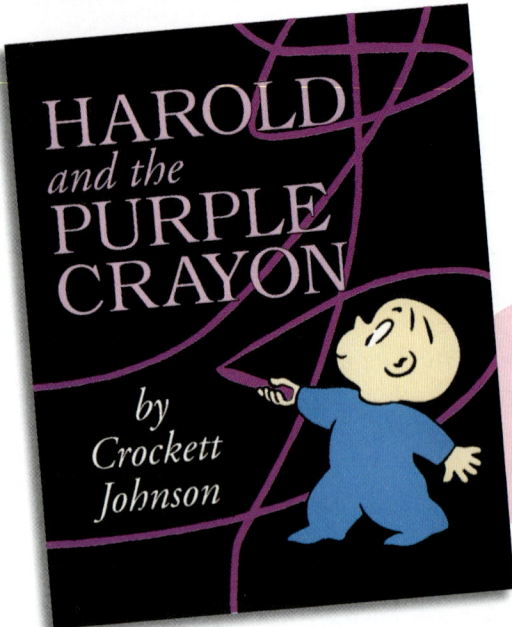

By Crockett Johnson

With a purple crayon in hand, Harold decides to take a walk in the moonlight. Since there isn't any moon, Harold draws one and begins his creation of the world around him—from the sidewalk to a boat to a pie—as he imagines his adventure.

Plentiful Purple Lines

Youngsters expand beyond crayons to make purple process art that Harold would be proud of!

Supplies

white construction paper
purple crayon
thick purple marker
thin purple marker
purple colored pencil

Steps

1. Choose a writing utensil.
2. Draw lines on the paper.
3. Repeat Steps 1 and 2 with other writing utensils.
4. Color sections of the drawing as desired.

ANYTIME

Hattie and the Fox

Written by Mem Fox
Illustrated by Patricia Mullins

When a nose pokes through nearby bushes, Hattie alerts her uninterested farm friends. As the hidden animal slowly reveals itself, Hattie becomes increasingly agitated, but her friends continue to disregard the situation—that is until Hattie declares that the animal is a fox!

It's a Fox!

There's a nose, two eyes, two ears, a body, four legs, and a tail hiding in this storytelling prop!

Supplies

white tagboard copy of the fox pattern on page 91
green tagboard bush cutout
jumbo craft stick
green tissue paper scraps
orange crayon
scissors
glue
utility knife (for teacher use only)

Setup

Cut a slit in the bush so the slit is slightly taller than the fox. Reinforce the slit with clear tape if desired.

Steps

1. Color the fox orange, leaving the chest fur and tip of the tail white.
2. Trim around the fox. Glue the craft stick to the fox as shown.
3. Glue tissue paper to the bush, keeping the paper flat near the slit.
4. Place the fox behind the bush and slide it through the slit.
5. Use the prop to retell the story.

If You Give a Mouse a Cookie

Written by Laura Joffe Numeroff
Illustrated by Felicia Bond

What happens when a boy shares a snack with a mouse? A lot! Once the mouse accepts the cookie, he makes himself at home and asks the boy for one thing after another. The boy quickly learns that taking care of the tiny critter is a huge job!

Snacktime for Mouse

This tasty looking snack is just too tempting for this little mouse!

Supplies

candy sprinkles (optional)
brown craft foam circle (cookie)
disposable cup
drinking straw
white facial tissue
large paper plate
brown mini pom-poms (chocolate chips)
large gray pom-pom (mouse)
length of gray yarn (tail)
2 mini wiggle eyes
glue

Steps

1. Drizzle glue inside the cup. Put the straw in the cup and add a few tissues (milk).
2. Glue the cup and the cookie to the plate.
3. Glue chocolate chips and sprinkles (optional) to the cookie.
4. Glue the mouse to the plate; then glue the eyes and tail to the mouse.

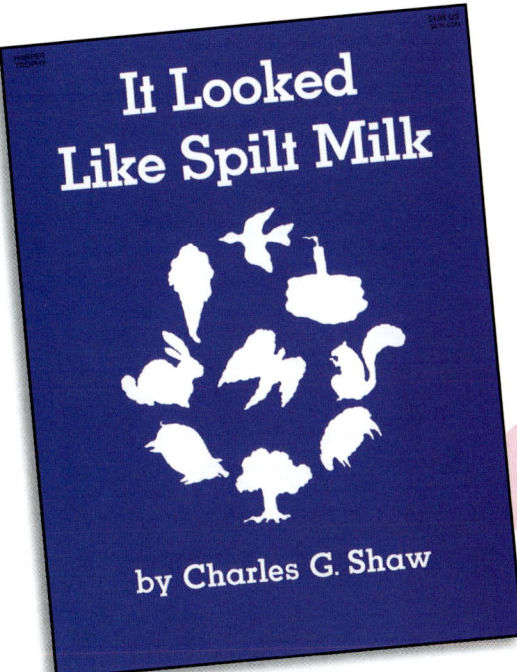

It Looked Like Spilt Milk

By Charles G. Shaw

What does the white shape look like? Sometimes spilt milk, sometimes a rabbit, and sometimes a bird. But if it isn't what it looks like, what could it be? It's a cloud!

A New Story

Bind youngsters' artwork together to create a class book similar to this classic story!

Supplies

gray construction paper
blue tempera paint
plastic spoon
black marker

Setup

Write the prompt "It looked like" on the gray paper. To make a final page for the class book, follow the steps below to make your own paint splotch. Then write "But it was just a puddle on the sidewalk!" on your paper.

Steps

1. Fold the gray paper in half.
2. Unfold the paper and use a spoon to drizzle blue paint near the fold.
3. Refold the paper and smooth it with your hand.
4. Unfold the paper and look at the paint splotch. Decide what it looks like and write (or dictate) the words.

Stack the completed pages with your page in the back. Then bind them together as desired. Read the finished book aloud to youngsters and then place the book in your classroom reading center.

ANYTIME

Little Blue and Little Yellow

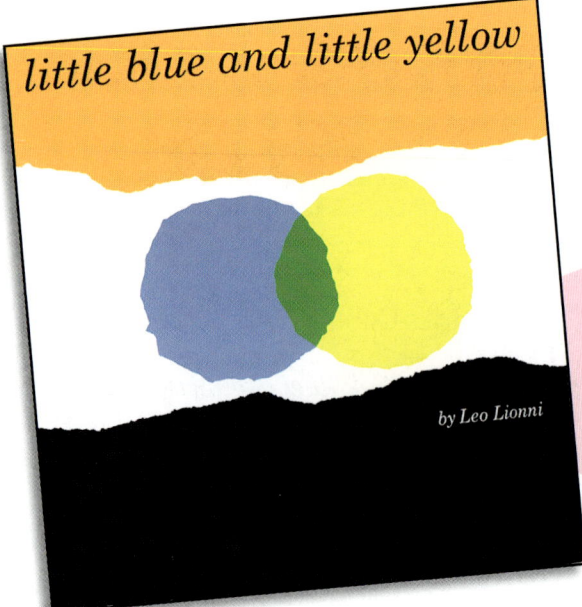

By Leo Lionni

Little Blue and Little Yellow are best friends. They play games and go to school together. But one day, they can't find one another. When they finally do meet, they are overjoyed and hug until they become green!

Hug Until You're Green!

Little Blue and Little Yellow meet again in this color-changing activity!

Supplies

2 lidded film canisters (or corks)
fingerpaint paper
blue and yellow fingerpaint, on separate paper plates

Steps

1. Dip a canister in paint and then press it on the paper. Repeat, adding more paint to the canister as needed.

2. Repeat Step 1 with the remaining canister and color of paint, making sure to have some of the circles "hug" to change the color.

ANYTIME

Mouse Paint

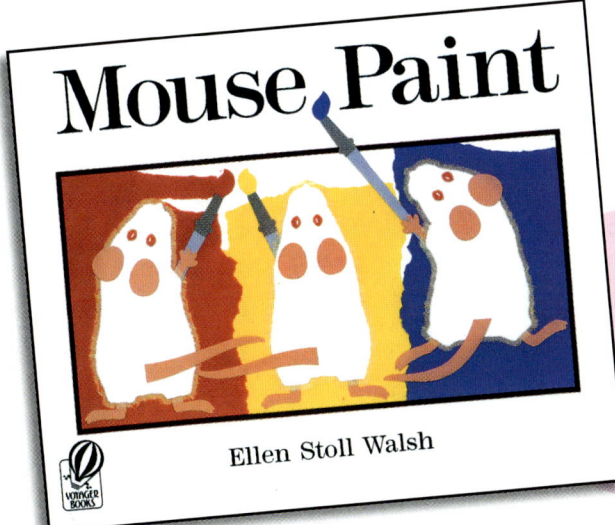

By Ellen Stoll Walsh

Three white mice on a piece of white paper are safely hidden from a cat. When they find three jars of colorful paint, they enjoy dancing in the paint and mixing colors. But they decide that it's better to paint the paper instead of themselves, as long as they leave some of the paper white!

Mischievous Mouse

This handmade mouse makes an adorable paint tool!

Supplies
white baby sock
plastic grocery bag
rubber band
plastic spoon
pink felt strip (tail)
white construction paper
red, yellow, and blue tempera paint
pink and black markers

Setup
Stuff the grocery bag into the sock. Tuck one end of the tail into the sock; then secure the tail and the opening with the rubber band. Draw eyes, ears, and a nose on the resulting mouse.

Steps
1. Spoon two colors of paint onto the paper.
2. Have the mouse scurry through the paint to mix the colors.

Tell About It! See page 93.

ANYTIME

My Friend Rabbit

By Eric Rohmann

Rabbit means well, but wherever he goes, trouble seems to follow. When Rabbit gets Mouse's airplane stuck in a tree, he coaches large animals to stand on top of one another so he can hold Squirrel up to reach the plane. The animal ladder tumbles, but the plane is freed. Mouse forgives his friend, even though trouble will soon follow again!

Up, Up, and Away!

This little plane looks like Mouse's plane. No doubt youngsters will be more successful pilots than Rabbit!

Supplies

small cardboard tube
2 jumbo craft sticks
string
red paint
yellow paint
paintbrushes
utility knife (for teacher use only)

Setup

Use the utility knife to cut two pairs of slits on opposite sides of the tube.

Steps

1. Paint the tube and craft sticks as desired with red and yellow paint. Allow them to dry.

2. Insert the craft sticks into the slits and slide them into place so they resemble the wings on a plane.

3. Tie the string to the plane, with help as needed.

4. Hold the string to make the plane fly.

Olivia

By Ian Falconer

Olivia is a lively piglet with boundless energy. She builds a sand castle skyscraper, paints a modern masterpiece, and challenges everyone else to keep up with her. She's a handful, but her parents still love their tireless little piggy!

Modern Masterpiece

Youngsters make a masterpiece similar to Olivia's with this engaging process art!

Supplies

red construction paper
red paint
black paint
white paint
white glue
craft sticks

Setup

Make a supply of glue paint by mixing each color of paint with an equal portion of glue. (Glue paint gives the project a thicker, more appealing texture.)

Steps

1. Dip a craft stick into a paint mixture and then drip, drizzle, and swirl the paint over the surface of the paper.
2. Repeat Step 1 with other colors of paint.

ANYTIME

Russell the Sheep

By Rob Scotton

Russell is a sheep that can't sleep. He tries everything he knows: pulling his nightcap over his eyes, trying different locations, and counting things. Finally, he decides to count the other sheep in his flock and nods off just as dawn breaks and the other sheep awaken.

It's Russell!

Students design eye-catching nightcaps for Russell look-alikes!

Supplies

large white construction paper oval (head)
small white construction paper oval (ears)
construction paper triangle (cap)
pom-pom
bingo daubers
markers, including black
scissors
crayons
glue

Steps

1. Use a black marker to draw a letter *V* (nostrils) and eyes on the head.
2. Cut the small oval in half lengthwise and attach the halves to either side of the head to make ears.
3. Use the daubers, markers, and crayons to decorate the cap. Attach the pom-pom to the top of the cap.
4. Glue the cap to the head.

Swimmy

Written by Leo Lionni

Unlike his red brothers and sisters, Swimmy is a little fish that is black as a mussel shell. When a tuna fish gobbles up all the little red fish, Swimmy sets out to explore the ocean. He finds a school of red fish that are too frightened to come out of hiding. But Swimmy teaches this school to work together to overcome danger!

Swimmy's World

Create a beautiful underwater scene similar to Swimmy's setting with paper doily rubbings!

Supplies
paper doily cut into several pieces
white copy paper
unwrapped crayons
tape

Steps

1. Arrange the doily pieces on a tabletop so they resemble an ocean floor and coral. Use rolled tape to lightly attach the arrangement to the table.

2. Place the paper atop the scene. Rub desired crayons over the doily arrangement.

3. Remove the paper and rub the remainder of the page with a blue crayon.

4. Use the crayons to draw fish and other sea life.

Where the Wild Things Are

By Maurice Sendak

A mischievous boy named Max is sent to his room. Soon afterward, his room transforms into a forest and Max "travels" to the land where the wild things are. Much to Max's delight, he is named king, and he has a grand time cavorting with the creatures. But in the end, Max is lonely and returns home—the place where he is loved best of all!

Private Boat

Travel along to where the wild things are with a personalized boat of your own!

Supplies

trimmed photo of yourself
paper plate half (boat)
large and small construction paper triangles (sails)
jumbo craft stick (mast)
tempera paint
paintbrush
markers
glue

Steps

1. Paint the boat. Let the paint dry.
2. Glue the sails to the mast.
3. Glue the photo and the mast to the boat.
4. Use the markers to add your name and desired details to the boat.

Tell About It!
See page 94.

Farm Animal Patterns
Use with "Who's in the Barn?" on page 64.

Name _____

Responding to literature

Bunny Cakes

Tell About It!

This is one way Max tells the grocer he wants Red-Hot Marshmallow Squirters:

Storytime Arts & Crafts • ©The Mailbox® Books • TEC61404

Note to the teacher: Use with page 66. Have each child write, illustrate, or dictate a response below the prompt. Then invite him to use markers and craft materials to decorate the cake.

86

Name _____

Responding to literature

Chicka Chicka Boom Boom

Tell About It!

What happens in the story?

Note to the teacher: Use with page 67. Have each child color the coconut tree and write to describe what happens in the story. Then have her color the coconut tree and glue on brown pom-poms (coconuts).

Storytime Arts & Crafts • ©The Mailbox® Books • TEC61404

Name _____ Responding to literature

Click Clack Moo: Cows That Type

Tell About It!

Here is the part I like best:

Storytime Arts & Crafts • ©The Mailbox® Books • TEC61404

Note to the teacher: Use with page 68. Have each child write, illustrate, or dictate a response.

Overalls Pattern
Use with "Designer Overalls" on page 70.

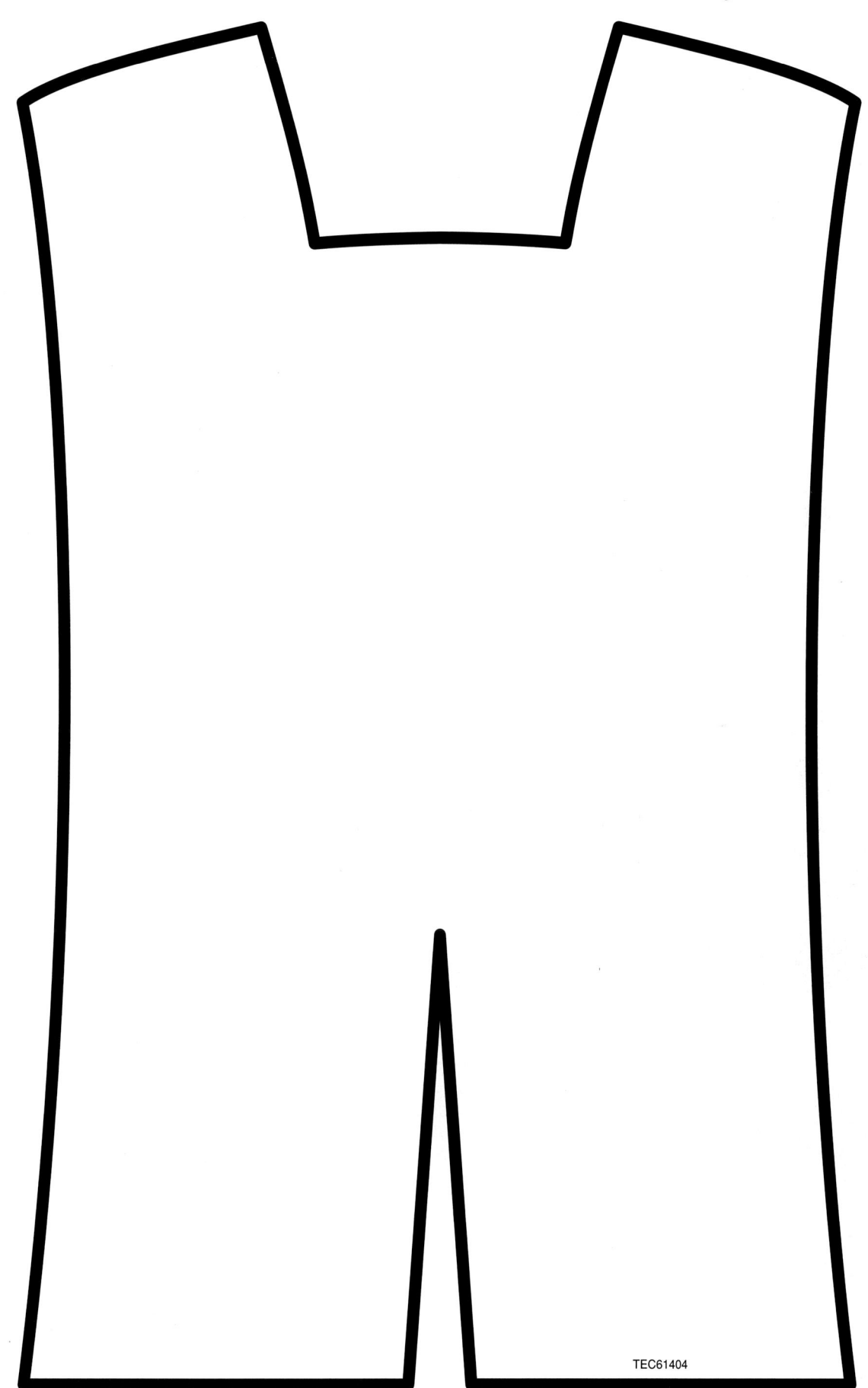

Responding to literature

Name _____

The Gruffalo

Tell About It!

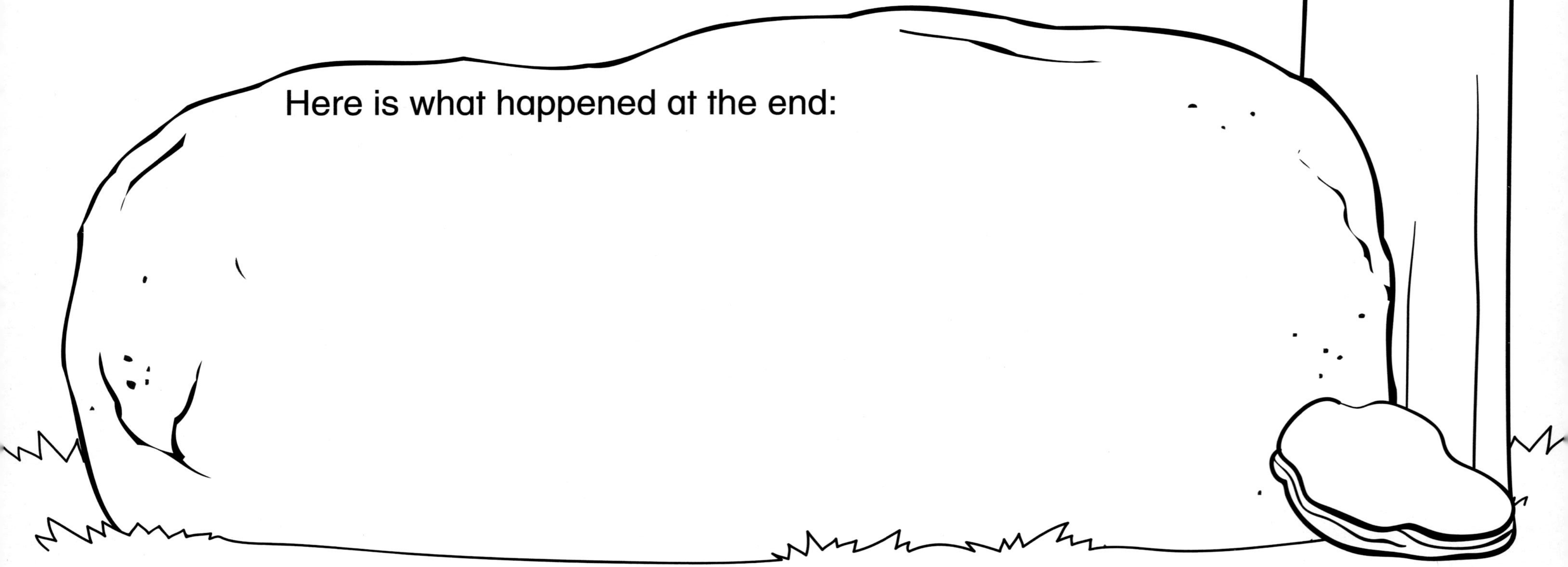

Here is what happened at the end:

_____
_____
_____

Note to the teacher: Use with page 73. Have each child write, illustrate, or dictate a response.

Storytime Arts & Crafts • ©The Mailbox® Books • TEC61404

Fox Pattern

Use with "It's a Fox!" on page 75.

Name _____   Responding to literature

If You Give a Mouse a Cookie

Tell About It!

The part I like best is:

Note to the teacher: Use with page 76. Have each child write, illustrate, or dictate a response. Invite her to rub a brown crayon around the writing or illustration and then glue brown mini pom-poms to the cookie. If desired, display students' work with a glass of milk cutout and the title "Beware if You Give a Mouse a Cookie!"

Name _____ Responding to literature

Mouse Paint

Tell About It!

This is what happens after the mice find the paint:

Name _____

Responding to literature

Where the Wild Things Are

Tell About It!

This is what happened when Max met the wild things:

___

Note to the teacher: Use with page 84. Have each child write, illustrate, or dictate a response. Then invite him to color the rest of the page.

Storytime Arts & Crafts • ©The Mailbox® Books • TEC61404

Title Index

Apple Pie Tree, The, 7

Bear Snores On, 27

Big Fat Hen, 63

Big Red Barn, 64

Blueberries for Sal, 56

Brown Bear, Brown Bear, What Do You See?, 65

Bunny Cakes, 66

Carrot Seed, The, 36

Chicka Chicka Boom Boom, 67

Click, Clack, Moo: Cows That Type, 68

Cookie's Week, 69

Corduroy, 70

Don't Let the Pigeon Drive the Bus!, 71

Down by the Bay, 53

Eggbert: The Slightly Cracked Egg, 39

Emperor's Egg, The, 28

First Day of Winter, The, 20

Fish Eyes: A Book You Can Count On, 54

Foot Book, The, 72

Froggy Goes to School, 6

Gingerbread Friends, 21

Go Away, Big Green Monster!, 9

Gruffalo, The, 73

Harold and the Purple Crayon, 74

Hattie and the Fox, 75

Hello, Ocean, 52

If You Give a Mouse a Cookie, 76

In the Tall, Tall Grass, 50

It Looked Like Spilt Milk, 77

Jump, Frog, Jump! 51

Kissing Hand, The, 5

Little Blue and Little Yellow, 78

Little Mouse, the Red Ripe Strawberry, and the Big Hungry Bear, The, 57

Little Scarecrow Boy, The, 12

Make Way for Ducklings, 40

Miss Rumphius, 38

Mitten, The, 22

Mouse Paint, 79

Mouse's First Spring, 35

My Friend Rabbit, 80

Olivia, 81

Owl Babies, 13

Owl Moon, 23

Planting a Rainbow, 37

Plump and Perky Turkey, A, 14

Polar Express, The, 26

Pumpkin Circle: The Story of a Garden, 10

Rain, 41

Rainbow Fish, The, 55

Runaway Bunny, The, 42

Russell the Sheep, 82

Snow, 24

Snowmen at Night, 25

Swimmy, 83

Tacky the Penguin, 29

Ten Red Apples, 8

Very Busy Spider, The, 11

Very Hungry Caterpillar, The, 43

Waiting for Wings, 44

Where the Wild Things Are, 84

Author Index

Archambault, John, 67

Baker, Keith, 63

Bateman, Teresa, 14

Brett, Jan, 21, 22

Brown, Margaret Wise, 12, 42, 64

Buehner, Caralyn, 25

Carle, Eric, 11, 43

Cooney, Barbara, 38

Cronin, Doreen, 68

Donaldson, Julia, 73

Ehlert, Lois, 37, 44, 54

Emberley, Ed, 9

Falconer, Ian, 81

Fleming, Denise, 20, 50

Fox, Mem, 75

Freeman, Don, 70

Hall, Zoe, 7

Hutchins, Pat, 8

Jenkins, Martin, 28

Johnson, Crockett, 74

Kalan, Robert, 41, 51

Krauss, Ruth, 36

Lester, Helen, 29

Levenson, George, 10

Lionni, Leo, 78, 83

London, Jonathan, 6

Martin, Bill, Jr., 65, 67

McCloskey, Robert, 40, 56

Numeroff, Laura Joffe, 76

Penn, Audrey, 5

Pfister, Marcus, 55

Raffi, 53

Rohmann, Eric, 80

Ross, Tom, 39

Ryan, Pam Muñoz, 52

Scotton, Rob, 82

Sendak, Maurice, 84

Seuss, Dr., 72

Shaw, Charles G., 77

Shulevitz, Uri, 24

Thompson, Lauren, 35

Van Allsburg, Chris, 26

Waddell, Martin, 13

Walsh, Ellen Stoll, 79

Ward, Cindy, 69

Wells, Rosemary, 66

Willems, Mo, 71

Wilson, Karma, 27

Wood, Audrey, 57

Wood, Don, 57

Yolen, Jane, 23